Imagine We Travel

By Jim Watrous

Sleepy Boy Books, P O Box 629, Madera, California 93639

ISBN-13:9781499699869

ISBN-10:1499699867

Introduction

A few seconds into any story, my Dad will interrupt me and ask, "Now Jim, is this a true story?"

I usually reply, "Not exactly, but if it didn't happen this way, it should have."

So be assured, I am married to Anna and have been for over 40 years and we do live in Madera, California and we did visit Hawaii and the Dominican Republic. In fact, we have made three such trips to that Caribbean island and elements of all three journeys are included in this story.

But there have been some artistic embellishments. The essence of the story is true, but names have been changed, some people are characterizations of two or three individuals combined into one, others have been "moved" to different places and times. Oh yes, and some events have been combined for the sake of the story. As for the places, I'm not imaginative enough to create them.

Some sections of this book are, of course, entirely fictional and are easily identified as such. That's the "imagine" part.

1

Preparing to Depart

Afew days before I set off to the Caribbean to meet up with my wife, Anna, and spend a few days in paradise, I took my Dad to his doctor appointment. The years, the sun and factors far beyond my comprehension have cursed him with spots on his quite bald head and, in two recent sessions, those "cancer spots" have been removed.

There is no mistaking that we are related. I have his "haircut" and his build. We also share this almost overwhelming desire to take center stage. Even at 86 years old, Dad has this need to welcome anyone who walks into the waiting room and to, in some small way, entertain them. I recognize these traits in myself immediately, but, most of the time, push them to one side.

I have been in a courtroom, waiting for the session to begin and have stood up in front of jittery audience and then, using a book as a prop, announced, "Ladies and gentlemen, we will begin in just a few minutes. Until then, we will continue with our reading. As those of you here yesterday will recall, we had reached Chapter Six, in which Dorothy faces an emotional crisis when her beloved neighbor, Stanley, is shipped off to the Hospital for the Criminally Insane and has left his imaginary dog, Clyde, in her care."

The people gaped at me. The clerk rolled her eyes. The bailiff sighed, "Not today, Jim."

My role in the care of our aging father is to handle some transportation chores and to provide entertainment. My younger brother Wayne and his wife Shelah shouldered a lot of responsibility when Dad was widowed for the second time and now my sister Peggy and her husband Randy are there for the heavy jobs.

We took the Avenue 12 off ramp, where a lot of work is being done in preparation for the high speed rail that will someday transform travel from Northern to Southern California. It wasn't long before we reached Highway 41 and turned south, crossed the San Joaquin River and were close to our destination.

We arrived right on time and took our seats in the waiting room. I looked around for a television set, tuned perhaps to a group of women discussing "hot topics" like Miley Cyrus or the Middle East. It's not as if I've been backstage, but I suspect that these shows are scripted much like professional wrestling. The ladies come out of their corners, throw a few jabs, eventually get tangled up in combat until the "bell" sounds and they go to commercial. Off the air, the cast relaxes and says, "Hey, you got me good that time."

But there was no TV at this place. Instead, they had an endless video playing interviews with health professionals on subjects ranging from Botox to toenail fungus. The audience, eight people including Dad and I, ignored the show completely. Meanwhile, the bouncy rhythm of a country song lightened the mood behind the counter. I'd taken a seat on a couch some distance away from the group and no one came in, so Dad was freed from his self-imposed role as master of ceremonies.

When the door to the back flew open and a woman said, "William," Dad jumped about a foot. That's usual these days. Any sudden sound or quick movement and he's startled. Then he looks around and plaintively asks for an explanation. I can clearly remember it being the other way around when we were both younger. He'd sneak up on me and ask, "What are you doing?" or "What are you thinking about?" I'd yelp and begin yammering. I didn't think I'd ever miss those moments, but, in a way, I do.

His visit with the doctor ended quickly and Dad came back to the waiting room smiling, thanking everyone for being so nice to him. In the car, he repeated that they treat him very well and, maybe sensing my reply, said, "I know they get paid to be nice, but still..."

There was a time when Dad and I argued about everything. In fact, that very comment would be fodder for some kind of back and forth, but we've both changed. As we drove back to Madera, I told him about an episode of "Maverick" I saw the other afternoon. "It turns out," I said, "that every ear of corn has an even number of rows."

"Are you sure?" he asked. I assured him it was. In fact, Maverick won a horse betting on that fact. Dad said he didn't remember the show so I sang the theme for him. He laughed and shook his head. "The stuff you come up with..."

"By the way, I'll be leaving in a couple of days for the Dominican Republic."

"Oh my, my, my."

If it sounds as if I sprung this news on him at almost the last possible moment, that's true. And we all tend to do that because it lessens the amount of time he worries. I could tell the process had begun.

"When will you be back? Because I'll be so relieved when you're back home."

"To be honest, so will I."

On our way from North Fresno to Madera, Dad and I dropped into a café in a little community called The Ranchos. It's basically one wide street with stores on both sides of the road and homes scattered on acre lots hidden beyond that one street.

The people who set up this eatery had a nostalgic theme in mind. The juke box played tunes from my childhood but my father, only 20 years older than I, had never heard most of them. At some point, I think he stopped listening to the radio. It might have been once he and Mom had children.

We were just about the only customers and that gave Dad a great opportunity to flirt with the waitress, who seemed to enjoy the attention. Both Mom and Marilyn, Dad's second wife, are fast asleep, awaiting resurrection, so I guess I shouldn't begrudge him this moment.

Still…

"Say Dad, this place reminds me of Eddie's Café up in Los Banos. It's actually owned by a guy named Larry. Now the interesting thing is that, when the café was on Sixth Street, there was a market across the street, Larry's Market, and it was owned by a man named Eddie."

"Jim, is that true?"

My mind traveled back to a recent visit to Los Banos and pretty soon my mouth was spouting forth on the subject.

The rising sun at my back cast a spotlight in front of my little red car as I ventured west on Highway 152 to the town of Los Banos. Once again, crime paid off, at least for me, in the form of a day's employment at the court as an interpreter.

That Friday morning, rush hour traffic played out before me as I came up to the first set of stoplights. No matter which way I went, there would be a line of cars and trucks, so I patiently waited to be able to turn right on Mercy Springs Road and then left on B Street in order to catch a glimpse of our old house. It appeared to be vacant.

My traffic strategy was based on more than nostalgia. Hours of thought on the subject has led me to these conclusions:

First of all, avoid schools.

Secondly, if you can't find a way around that situation, at least try and make it an elementary school. The reason is that children are led across the street in bunches, not allowed to trickle, one by one, glaring at you in defiance, making life just as miserable for you as it appears to be for them.

There are two other factors that suggest taking an alternative route. The school bus driver has been given enormous power. With just a flick of a switch, red lights can be activated that paralyze the movement of other cars and keep them frozen in position. Then, there are the parents who have driven their progeny to the campus and, not content with having them bail out of the vehicle and walk briskly into the waiting arms of the educational system, insist on trading last-minute instructions with them. "Now, don't forget..." "Remember what I told you..." "You promised to..." "No matter what, mister, you..."

Once past the school, your ordeal is not over. All those cars have to go somewhere and, is it my imagination, or do they really seem to be conspiring to keep me at a stop sign for as long as possible? Finally, I have to do what I swear is the latest stupid thing. Instead of turning, I merge. Turning consists of waiting until all is clear and then pulling out. Merging is waiting for an opening and then bursting from the starting blocks, hoping the approaching driver will take mercy on you and slow down a bit.

When I went through this entire routine with one of the bailiffs at the Los Banos court, he summarized the situation much more succinctly. "Ten pounds of poop in a five-pound bag." That, my friend, is the essence of poetry.

Los Banos has always attracted a cosmopolitan crowd. When we lived there from roughly 1979 to 1987, I met people who'd come from different points on the globe, many of them to help build or maintain the San Luis Dam. Working for the local newspaper, The Enterprise, I met such characters as, "The Singing Pig Farmer." This was not an insult hurled at him by others, but the title of his album, a recording of songs he'd sung to his herd over the years.

Then, there was Vincent Hillyer, the ex-brother-in-law of the Shah of Iran. Yes, he had married into the royal family, the one described as "sitting on the Peacock Throne," quite a visual to be sure, but things hadn't gone well and he and the Shah's sister split up. He ended up in Los Banos, living with his mother (a wonderful woman). When the Iranian hostage crisis happened, Vincent got on television and in the pages of our newspaper on a regular basis. He had some insights into the reasons for this animosity between the Ayatollah and the Shah.

Vincent also had a connection to Transylvania, that spot in Europe closely associated with the legend of Dracula, and he would explain the whole megilla every year around Halloween.

(Let me pause and give you the benefit of my having opened the wonderful old book, *"Hooray for Yiddish,"* by Leo Rosten, to the word "megilla," which he defines as, among other more religious meanings, "the same old familiar story or excuses." An example: "On and on she yakked until, after 15 minutes of this *megilla*, she paused to exclaim, 'You know something, Rabbi? I came in with the most terrible headache of my whole life and it just disappeared!' The rabbi sighed, 'No, your headache didn't disappear. I have it.'")

Don Hughes was another local who had a great story to tell. He'd been an airplane mechanic up in the San Francisco area. At night, he bowled and did so with such astonishing ability that he was tempted to become a professional. One night, the lanes were closed for repairs and Don was walking back to his car in disgust when he spotted a store devoted to model railroading. He went in, became fascinated with the hobby, and got started on a set-up in his own house.

Over the next few months, he bowled less and built more pieces for his railroad. When he finished, he did what many people in that avocation do. He photographed it all. That sent him in yet another direction as he tried out different cameras and lenses, tripods and lighting arrangements. Pretty soon, the model railroad town lost its hold on him and Don started taking pictures instead. And that's the hobby that became his profession to this day.

Patiently waiting for the Spanish speakers to be hailed before the honorable bench, I thought about those guys and the town they called home, wondered if the Pig Farmer and the ex-brother-in-law were still around, planned to stop by Don Hughes' studio downtown and daydreamed about what might have happened if we hadn't made the move to Madera some 27 years ago.

"Maintenance required," the yellow light on my dashboard insisted. When the advisory was in the form of flashing, I took it to mean that, if the car's engine ever needed some attention, this would be the exact place it would be posted.

But now, the light was not intermittent, but constant. I got the message. "Maintenance required."

That's why, after dropping off Dad at his house not far from my own, I ended up in the service bay at one of those oil change places where the technicians circle your car, shouting gibberish to one another.

"Seventy-eleven empirical status in bay two!" is what I hear.

"Umptity, repitity, rah!" someone replies.

But they do a nice job.

The only part of the process where there seemed to be some incompetence was behind the steering wheel. It started when I tried to drive forward. I could just see my car slipping into the big hole in the middle of the driveway. If the young man waved me one way, I practically swerved over in that direction. He tried to get me back on track and I yanked the wheel the other way.

Finally, I was in the right position and ready for my car to be serviced.

Then, after being reminded that they won't try to sell me anything, the young men, one by one, came up to the window, usually with a visual aid in hand. "As you can see, sir, the fluid that governs your ratchet driver has turned this color when it should be like this. Your mileage indicates also that it should be changed. It's only..."

My policy is to look the technician right in the eye and ask, "What do you think?"

Their policy is to look me right in the eye and say, "I think you should buy this product."

When I do decline something, I blame my wife.

"I'm going to have to tell her I turned something down," I told this befuddled teenager. "This fuel injection elixir will have to be that thing."

He turned on his heel with a curt, "Thank you sir," but I felt he was displeased with more than just the state of my car's engine.

The worst part came when I was asked for an opinion. "Sir, are your windshield wipers in good condition?" or "Sir, will you want your tires inflated at the manufacturer's recommended level?"

"Wipers?" I squeaked. "Wipers?" Yes, I see the wipers. "I think you installed them last time."

And, miraculously, I was right!

"Correct sir!"

I sat up a little straighter. "And the tires? They are at 40 lbs. and they are recommended to be 30 lbs. pressure."

Why, this was troubling. "How did that happen?" I blurted out.

The young man was on the verge of saying something hilarious at my expense, but he held back.

"You know," I hastened to explain, "I thought I had a flat tire, so I had them checked at this place down the road and it was me that insisted they add air to all of them. They just looked low to me."

This was a recurring theme in my life. Ignorance of mechanical matters makes me suspicious. A couple of weeks ago, the garage door, while cascading down, suddenly seemed to snap and plummeted the rest of the way, landing on the pavement with a screeching sound.

There is a big tag on the inside of the door that warns homeowners from trying to fix such problems themselves. In fact, we had a friend try to do that and he ended up in the hospital emergency room with a big gash in his arm. So, we made the telephone call and the man from the garage door company came out. I led him around to the sliding glass door and was rearranging a few boxes I'd cleared away when I heard him say, "All taken care of."

He'd pulled on the cord, which I had done as well, but not in the trained, professional way it takes to get the job done. He listened wearily to my long explanation and said, "I'll service the door just to make the trip worth it for you."

Back at the oil change place, the other two bays were clear so I had four technicians huddled over my open hood, with an occasional, "Pardon the intrusion," when they sprayed the door locks or checked a filter behind the glove compartment. The shouting reached a crescendo. I thought they were getting ready to launch me into space rather back on Gateway Drive but, to be honest, all the attention was flattering.

The total amount was tallied, presented to me and I did my part by signing a few papers. I thanked them for the bottled water and was about to bid them farewell when it dawned on me.

"Pardon me," I called out, "but could you turn off this maintenance required light."

There is a trick to it. You turn the key with one hand and push a button with the other and, then, the light flickers and goes dark.

"You mean, I could have just done that instead of all this?" I laughed. The team dutifully smiled as if none of them had ever heard that line before.

Toodling down Yosemite Avenue with my car's motor purring, I concentrated on my driving. If you ever come upon me on the road, don't expect a friendly beep because I don't see you. Hands at ten and two, jaw thrust forward, I motor on. Music or some radio talk show might waft around my ears, but my mind is set on just getting where I'm going. If not, things don't go well. It's not that I'm a bad driver, just an easily distracted one. Especially when I am in uncharted waters.

2

Bound for Paradise

It was "getaway day," time to gather up my luggage and set out for the "far side of the world," as one of the poets said. My itinerary called for me to take off from Fresno quite early in the morning and land in Los Angeles at a decent hour, wait a few hours and then board a bigger jet to Dallas, Texas.

I would arrive at this transportation hub in the evening, have to stay overnight and then, early the next morning, continue my journey in a plane to Miami, Florida. After about a day's wait in The Sunshine State, I would be ushered into an airplane for the final leg, the one to Santiago de los Caballeros in the northern part of the Dominican Republic.

That's where I would rendezvous with my wife Anna and we would be whisked away to this fabulous, all-inclusive resort for a few days before returning to Santiago for another week or so with two of our friends, Missy and Priti, who had moved there a few years ago.

Reader, you are justified in asking, "Isn't that a long way around the block?" And you would be right, but I was "traveling on miles," which meant the airlines were willing for me to take advantage of their offer, but I'd have to do it their way.

For the longest time, I thought that if you had 40,000 miles, for example, it meant you could fly 40,000 miles. How naïve. But I wasn't complaining.

After Anisa and Amanda gave me a hearty farewell, I went through the process of getting to the gate. The relatively big bag was checked in and the other accompanied me through security. I was invited to pose for a second to make sure I was no danger to anyone and then I waved goodbye to my two daughters and walked to the very end of the terminal to find my gate.

On a chair, I saw that day's copy of the Fresno Bee and scanned the Classified Ads just out of curiosity. What I found convinced me there is no lack of material for a story-teller. Some of the items for sale simply cried out for attention.

"Belt Buckle," one read, "Says bull---- $20" What would possess someone to buy such an article and, having once made that decision, back away from it?

"Chains, snow tire, used once, $20." Now there's a story. I know because it happened to me. Crossing the mountains in Southern Oregon into Northern California in an unexpected flurry, I spent a few terrifying minutes trying to get the chains on. If it weren't for a truck driver who took pity on me, we'd have been up there until the spring thaw.

"Singing Bowl, Striker, Stand Yoga," and I had no idea what they were talking about.

Under "Antiques, Art and Collectibles," there was a collection of Camel cigarette ashtrays and a Diego Rivera print, "Flower Vendor." I can see where the Rivera fits in, but ashtrays? How old does something have to be to attain the status of antique?

As for the other sections of the newspaper or the miles of items available online, I recall having lunch with Walter Cronkite the other day. Of course, the venerable newsman died quite a few years ago, but his book, "*A Reporter's Life,*" was propped up on the dining room table and, in it, he told a story that might be instructive to this day.

Not long after World War II, Cronkite and several other journalists were sent to Moscow to dispatch stories about Soviet life. In order to provide him with transportation and perhaps just to make sure he didn't wander too far off on his own, Cronkite was given a car and driver named Alexander.

"He was a regular 15-minute newscast every day," Uncle Walter wrote. "He had been a driver in the Soviet army and, during our first months together, he spent most of our conversation time praising the American 'zheep,' as he called it." Alexander thought the Jeep won the war for the Allies. As the "drumbeat of propaganda" continued daily through all media in Russia, the driver began to change his tune. "Within months, he was asking me, plaintively and with genuine disappointment, why we Americans claimed to have invented the *zheep* when we knew the Russians had." He told Cronkite that the U.S. switched the nameplates from the original Russian ones to carry off this deception.

The majority of what we call "news" today is not about something that happened, but what people say about things that happened. And the public is herded, one way or the other, according to individual preference, to believe separate and distinct versions of what started out as fact.

Putting down the paper, I thought back to a nostalgic morning of interpreting at Fresno Superior Court. I was assigned to the courtroom of His Honor Brant Bramer, whom I knew 15 years ago when he was an assistant district attorney. He and I spent many a pleasant day in front of Judge Gene Gomes. I particularly remember Bramer facing the audience and asking, "Are there any victims or family of victims present?" Hearing no reply (usually), he would gesture in my direction and I would say the same thing in Spanish.

One day, I told him that he had no way of knowing that for sure. "What I could be saying is that the following court proceeding is property of Fresno Superior Court and is solely for the entertainment of our audience. Any recording, recreation or description of what happens here without the express written permission of Mr. Bramer is prohibited."

A parade of familiar faces came through and plead their cases before Judge Bramer. Leroy Faulk told me a funny story about the attorney known as "Three Rivers" Logan. "He invited me to take a walk around his place," said Faulk, "and I kept running into shady characters with farm tools in their hands. They'd ask me who I was and what was I doing out there." I'm not sure if I was supposed to take that as a joke or not.

Another attorney stopped me in the hallway and asked, "Didn't you work in Madera?" When I confessed I had, he said, "Remember that case we did together?" I played along. "Of course. You won, didn't you?" Well, as a matter of fact, he did. The DA dismissed the case but the kid had to go through a mental health evaluation first. Turned out the craziest people involved were his relatives who got him mixed up in a burglary ring. The poor kid was worse than a bad lookout. He went out and told everybody who'd listen what they were all up to.

As the morning ended, I was standing next to a man who spoke Spanish and drove his car with a suspended license. Judge Bramer made sure the man knew his rights and I dutifully interpreted every word of the back and forth between them. Still, in that little corner of my mind reserved for such frivolity, a highlight reel of some of our moments in Gomes' court was playing. By the way the judge seemed to be trying to fight off a smile, I got the impression Brant Bramer was having a similar moment.

L ooking down after the jet took off from Fresno to at a glorious February sun beaming down on the southern San Joaquin Valley, I was pretty sure that I could see the small city of Visalia, so I thought about Tex Clevenger.

Growing up on Rogers St. in Madera, we didn't have a backyard big enough for a decent size baseball field so I convinced my brothers that we could still play if we used, let's say, the head of a doll stolen from my sister or an empty plastic lemon. In addition, we would have to adopt a whole set of rules that would cover base running and fielding. The final touch was "naming" ourselves after the players of the time. And whenever I needed a tough right-handed pitcher, a mean, surly, angry guy who wasn't afraid to come inside with the submarine ball, then I'd call on Tex Clevenger.

All I knew of the man I learned from the back of his baseball card. It told me that he was a native of the Visalia area, had signed with the Boston Red Sox in 1954 and then got traded to the old Washington Senators in 1955. In 1960, he was picked up by the California Angels but traded to the New York Yankees just in time for the glory years of 1961 and 1962. On the face side of the card, there was a photo of an angular face, unshaved for a few days, a cheek bulging with chewing tobacco and a scowl topped off with a cap set on his head in such a way as if to say, "Better not dig in."

Then, in the late 1990's, while working for the Madera Tribune, I heard that Tex Clevenger would be one of the "celebrities" at a golf tournament to raise money for

D.A.R.E., a "just say no" drug awareness program. So I went out to the links that Saturday morning and, after asking around for a while, ended up on a green where Tex Clevenger was hunched over a ball, measuring the distance to sink a putt for par.

I'm sure Tex was used to being interviewed about those Yankee teams, Mickey Mantle, Roger Maris and the 1962 World Series when Bobby Richardson broke our Giant hearts, but he wasn't prepared for my angle. I told him about Rogers St. and his baseball card and how I always brought him from the bullpen, just the way they did when he played for the Cleveland Indians.

"Cleveland?" he hooted. "That wasn't me. And I never threw a submarine ball." But I distinctly remembered how Tex would dip down, almost brushing the mound with his knuckles and then delivering a devastating fastball right in on the hands.

"You got me mixed up with someone else," Tex laughed, after inviting me to ride in his cart. "All I can tell you is that I did throw that pitch once in a while and because of my last name, some people do associate me with Cleveland, but..." Sure, of course. We both sat back and enjoyed the ride, satisfied that we had solved one of the little mysteries of the game.

That out of the way, I got down to the kind of interview Tex had given thousands of times. "Mickey Mantle was the best all around player I ever saw. He hit the 34th and 280th homeruns of his career off me. I know because someone sent me the baseballs to be autographed." Mantle, he said, would have been unstoppable if he hadn't suffered the knee injuries. "Sure, he drank a lot too, but hell, we all did back in those days," Tex chuckled, then turned serious, "But no drugs. Never."

After whacking the golf ball up to the green, Tex turned to me and said, "Ted Williams was the best hitter I ever saw and he wasn't at all like they said in the papers. A nice guy. He did a lot for the younger players, especially the pitchers, because he figured he'd be facing them later on."

"I was with the Senators and we were playing the Red Sox in Fenway Park. I got called in to face Williams and I thought I threw him three strikes and two balls. The umpire saw it as one strike and four balls. The next day, we were all standing around the batting cage and I asked Ted where that 2-1 pitch missed."

Tex put his thumb and forefinger out and they almost touched,. "Ted Williams said, 'Just that much inside,' and then I asked him about the 3-1 pitch and Ted said, 'That much outside.' And we all laughed and then he said, 'Hey Tex, why don't you ever throw me that dinky slider of yours?' I told him, 'I don't need it. I can get you out with my fastball.'"

That very afternoon, Tex continued, he was called in to face Williams again in a relief situation. "I decided to cross him up. As I came over the top with my slider, I looked down at the plate and there was Ted with a big grin on his face. He swung from the heels and the ball took off like a shot and went over the bullpen. That guy jumped up and down, yelling out at me, 'I knew you'd throw it to me!'"

"Johnny Pesky gave me the name Tex because he said I looked just like Tex Houston, who pitched for the Red Sox during the war years. The name stuck."

I asked him if there came a moment when he was on the mound in a major league park and it just struck him just how great it was. The thrill of having made it to a spot that so many other kids dreamed about.

"Oh yeah," he said, "I know exactly what you mean. It was the first time I pitched in Yankee Stadium, the second game of a series and I was the starter. We lost to Allie Reynolds, 5-3. My best starts? I threw a shutout, a six-hitter against Cleveland and then, with Washington, I started and we won, 6-0, and broke a 13-game losing streak. I think that's the day I broke Billy Martin's jaw."

I jumped back and pointed at him. "That's where I got the impression you threw high and tight."

"Sure I did. Everyone did back then. That pitch broke Billy's jaw in 14 places. A couple of days later, we had a rainout, so I went out to the hospital to see Martin. They took a photograph of us talking. Well, I was talking. Billy was mumbling."

"That guy would charge the mound every time he got hit. Not that time, of course, but usually."

As the golf round grew to a close, I just started throwing out names. Like Roger Maris...

"There's a Hall of Famer right there," Tex responded. "I saw his 61st home run in Yankee Stadium in 1961 from the bullpen. And, as a man, he was a great guy. Quiet, but not shy really, class all the way. Good outfielder, smart on the basepaths, not a strong arm, but an accurate one. He never got all the credit he deserved."

"How about Lenny Green?" I asked.

Tex smiled, "Naw, you mean Pumpsie Green. But you were close," and he held out his thumb and forefinger, "just that close."

Although I couldn't possibly see it even from that height, I knew Death Valley was out there somewhere. And I knew that, at that very moment, a couple from Madera would be there on their annual trip.

I once asked them why they do such a thing.

"The serenity," said the husband, Sam, "the quiet, the calm, to see the stars and listen to the coyotes and ravens."

His wife Brenda and their children Jaime and Jael went together for many years. I think Jaime and his wife Jacqueline still do, but Jael and her husband Josh now live in the Dominican Republic. "We used to go to Yosemite," said Brenda, "but we decided to go somewhere else because it was so cold up there at that time of year."

So Death Valley came to mind?

"Plenty warm," she said. "And we've been going back every year since."

"Every time we go, I see something new or I rediscover something and see it as if it were for the first time," her husband Sam chimed in.

Even before that first trip, Sam had this urge to see the place. "When I was a kid, I used to watch Death Valley Days on television and I always wanted to see it in person."

"Maybe I can explain it this way. You stand at the lowest point in the hemisphere, 284 feet below sea level, and look straight up to Telescope Peak. That's 9,000 feet high. The air is so clear that you feel as if the mountain had sprouted right up in front of you. It's part of the mystery of the place. You can't even believe your eyes. Like the old prospector said, 'Is this a mirage or just my imagination.'"

"Take the Racetrack, for example, where the rocks have obviously moved. You can see the trail they left behind. But how did it happen? Was there a hard rain and then gusts of wind so strong that the rocks were pushed along the sand? How do you explain the way they went in different directions?" Sam lifted his arms and spread out his palms, searching my face for some sign of appreciation. "No one really knows."

He ticked off the other places. "Devil's Golf Course, Titus Canyon, the Artist's Palette, Scotty's Castle... Now, he was a con man, a wild west performer and that castle of his was never completed."

Sam laughed. "That's why you don't go there in the summer. That's when the tourists from Europe want to go and they always take pictures of each other holding up a thermometer to prove they've been there when it's 135 degrees. When we go, always in mid to late February, it's only about 80 degrees."

Thinking that I might be tempted, Sam warned me, "When you go, don't take a metal detector. A friend of ours had one and they ended up prosecuting him for it. I tried to testify in his behalf at the trial but it seemed as if every time I opened my mouth, I just made it worse. He ended up paying a $60 fine and his lawyer cost him more than $1,000. I felt really bad about that."

It's 481 miles from Madera to Death Valley and I have never taken that ride, nor plan to. But Sam and Brenda will.

"I love it once I'm here, but I could do without the drive," Brenda admitted. "Once I'm there, it's so quiet and there's a million stars beaming down on you. Then I go and fall in love with the place all over again. Sam always makes us go to the Visitor Center slide show. Tell him why honey."

"At first," he said, "it was because I wanted to learn more about the place from the park rangers but then, after

I'd heard the same lecture a few times, I kept on going because it's the most peaceful place to take a nap you could ever want."

"When we were first married," Brenda added, "we didn't travel much. In fact, we didn't have a television set. Sam and I would play violin duets together for entertainment. The trouble is Sam has a tin ear so it must have sounded pretty awful to everyone else. Our Death Valley trips have become a tradition with us. We go to other places to be tourists and sightseers, but we go there for a different reason."

"To relax," Sam said.

But I heard more than those two words. What I heard was: To stand together beneath an enormous black sky dotted with a million stars, listening to the quiet and the calm and the ravens and the coyotes and then to lower their gaze to each other's eyes and find love in Death Valley again.

The flight attendant had obviously made this speech thousands of times before. In that distinctive Texas twang, she informed the passengers of the safety features of the gigantic jet we had all boarded headed east from Los Angeles.

Her tone did not betray what would come next, however. "Please put your electronic devices on airplane mode or pie a la mode. By the way, our pilot today is Charles Lindbergh and he will be coming through the cabin shortly. That's why we dim the lights, so you won't be frightened and it doesn't hurt the rest of the crew either."

Oh, a comedy routine.

"If you still get too clear a glimpse of our pilot, we did bring liquor aboard to help you cope. Anyway, I will be coming by from time to time to make sure your seat belts are fastened and your shoes match your outfits."

Since that early morning, I have actually seen a Youtube video of another flight attendant giving a similar performance and I have read that this is all done with the approval of the airline. It's an attempt to get passengers to pay attention during the important message concerning using the lavatory as a smoking room or moving around during turbulence or how to stay afloat if we have to ditch in the ocean. A few laughs. That should do the trick.

As we banked down into the Dallas area, the flight attendant resumed her standup routine by reading off a list of connecting flights. Scattered among them was a reference to Katmandu, for example, and we could get there by going to Gate 99. For some reason, that line stuck in my head long enough for me to win a bottle of wine.

She'd warned us there would be a pop quiz after her last set and, true to her word, offered either a bottle of red or white to anyone who could recall the gate number for Katmandu.

I took the white. But wine immediately gives me a headache. The liquid has not even reached my throat before my head starts throbbing. So, from the minute I got the bottle, I started planning on how to get rid of it.

Up close, the flight attendant, despite her obvious comedic talent, seemed quite stiff, formal and reminded me of a teacher who had been forced to "be nice to the students". Her gold name tag read, "Vimala," and I couldn't resist.

"Is that your first name or last?"

She eyed me coolly and shook her head. Having presented me with the white wine as if it were a major award, she straightened up and said, "No phone calls and no flowers, all right?"

"Oh no," I laughed. "Don't worry about that. I'm married. And for a long time. No, it's just that I have heard that first name before. In fact, there is a Vimala Method of handwriting. Did you know that?"

"You married guys are the worst ones and no, never heard of it. Have a nice flight. Enjoy your wine," and I was left with my thoughts, which were the following.

Back in 1996 and 1997, I wrote a column for a daily newspaper and the toughest part was coming up with something to fill that space every day, so I regularly scoured the pages of trade journals, out-of-town papers and the steady stream of mail coming into the office. That's how I found out about Loretta Thomas of Oakhurst, a "certified handwriting analyst," willing to teach the Vimala Method because its practitioners can "increase their self esteem and validate their self worth."

"I grew up in Bass Lake," she explained to me over the telephone, "and I graduated from Berkeley. Then I lived up in Sacramento for 20 years and had two daughters. I moved back to this area in 1989 and that's when I met Vimala Rodgers at a Valley Women's Conference. She wrote a book called, *Change Your Handwriting, Change Your Life*, and I ended up going to her school in Palo Alto called the Institute of Integral Handwriting Studies."

Mrs. Thomas continued, "The traditional methods like Palmer, Zaner-Bloser and D'Nealian all have these repressive strokes built into them. This method is different. Every moment you write will help you lose anger and frustration and become totally focused." And I could learn the joys of such moments for an investment of three hours and $25, "which will free your inner self, break bad habits and live with a freedom you have never known before."

It sounded great, but $25, eh?

"The response hasn't been very good so far," Mrs. Thomas acknowledged, "but I think it's just a matter of getting the word out."

The least I could do for my readers, the few there might be, was direct them to this freedom, this improved self worth and self esteem. Could she send me a brochure or flyer? And, without a trace of anger or frustration, Mrs. Thomas promised to do so.

Upon receipt of the materials, I took the idea to a fourth-grade teacher at Washington Elementary School in town. Mrs. Alexander listened attentively and then said, without much enthusiasm. "Well, I've been teaching for seven years and I haven't heard about this method. What I can tell you is that we teach cursive handwriting in the third grade and we perfect it in the fourth grade. My experience has been that there is not always a correlation between the way a child writes and his character."

"Some children are sloppy for no other reason than they lack motor skills," and she looked at me as if I were one of them. (I was.) "Others are artistically inclined and take a great deal of pride in having wonderful penmanship. Then there are others who are more concerned with content and they write as fast as they can without worrying much about how it looks." (Again, that's me.)

We chose a student, Alexis Ornelas, and I asked her to write the words, "Many years ago."

When she finished, I asked, "How do you feel?"

"Just fine," she said with a glance at her teacher.

"Now, try it this way," and I did my best to explain the 45 degree upstrokes rather than finishing off the letters by descending. "What do you think?" I asked when she wrote the words again.

"Naw," the girl said. "I don't like it."

And she walked away, never to experience the freedom, the exhilaration, the soaring self worth and self esteem embodied in the Vimala Method.

The passenger in the middle seat snapped me out of that memory, "May I?" he inquired and I said yes before knowing exactly what he had in mind. Up to that moment, he appeared to be unconscious. I couldn't determine his age except he was younger than me but old enough to have competed for that wine.

But now he leaned toward me, his hand extended and in between his thumb and forefinger, he held a tiny square, a cube really, and I guess he snapped a photograph. That was the last time he asked permission. From that point on, he'd suddenly come to life, stick his hand out past my chest and take another picture.

Maybe it was my imagination, but I thought he smelled. But I probably smelled too.

When we started our descent into Dallas, he attempted small talk. "If you need any help with that bottle of wine, let me know." I placed it in his free hand, the one without the camera.

"It's all yours."

In the half hour before landing in Dallas, I learned that the passenger next to me was a professional woodcarver who'd been to Los Angeles for a major showing of his work and, in the process, had attended his daughter's high school graduation.

"Her mom and I divorced when she was little. I moved back to Texas after that, but always kept up my child support payments, did what little extra I could on that score, visited her quite a bit. Her Mom never let her come back here though. Aw, I guess it was for the best. I'm remarried now 12 years. My ex has been pretty good about it, all things considered."

I understood perfectly what was going on. He was nervous about landing. I get the same way whenever I get blood drawn or the dental hygienist is just about to start shearing the plaque off my teeth.

He thought I was kidding about the wine, but I insisted and gave him my diagnosis. "I think it's the sulfates they use as a preservative," which is something I picked up from a source other than the wine industry.

He nodded. "I learned about carving from my grandfather here in Texas when I was only seven years old. He was whittler and just believed that everyone should know how to handle a knife. I'm not even the best carver in my family. My sister is. She's a science teacher in Missouri but exhibits at fairs and shows. Likes to carve mammals."

"My specialty is birds. I started with ducks. The first two were put on display at a barber shop in town and one of the guys there saw them and got me in touch with a professional woodcarver. He told me to sell them for $750 each and I couldn't believe it. I was pretty sure they'd sit there in the window for years at that price."

"Then the barber called me one day and said a guy was offering $1,000 for the two and what did he want me to do. I yelled into the phone, 'Take it! Take it now! Right now!' We still laugh about that."

"Hummingbirds are what I'm into now. Very popular for some reason. Hey, drive around and you'll see the feeders all over the place. People, especially older folks, just love hummingbirds."

"People are the most difficult thing to carve. Caricatures are different. But a real portrait has to be so fine, so precise. It's the toughest thing to carve."

The key, I was told as the plane touched down, was getting invited to compete in a show. "The guy who got me in the business was laid off at a dairy where he worked and took up woodcarving in a big way. And then he won

$35,000 first prize at a show. Never had to milk another cow in his life."

The woodcarver finally relaxed and leaned back as the plane taxied to the gate. "My wife's meeting me in the parking lot. You going on to somewhere else?"

"Katmandu," I chuckled. "No. Dominican Republic."

And, with a wave of the wine bottle, my seat mate departed.

As I made my way to a nearby hotel to grab a few hours of sleep before catching the next day's flight to Miami, my mind traveled with Robbie Stiggins (the name I'd decided to assign to my fellow passenger, the woodcarver).

His wife of 12 years, the former Cathy Jahrleeng, fiddled with her cell phone after getting his text that the plane had landed and he would be out to the short term parking lot "directly." It wasn't too cold outside, so she turned off the engine and sat behind the wheel, tapping out a random rhythm with her fingers.

A boy she had known since high school took her to a woodcarving show as his idea of a date. That's where she bumped into Robbie. Serious, artistic, brooding, obviously recently devastated by some heartbreak, it was all too much to resist.

The shuttle bus roared into view and soon the doors flipped open and people started hauling their suitcases and boxes into view. Cathy recognized Robbie by his slouch and gait, an old duffel bag thrown over his left shoulder. In his right hand, he carried a small wine bottle and waved it in her direction. As he got closer, Robbie nodded for her to reach across and open the passenger door.

She did and her husband slung his bag over the front seat and it landed with a thud in the middle of the back seat. He placed the bottle between them and then leaned over and gave her the kind of kiss you expect from people married a while.

"Guy next to me won this in a stupid contest. I was asleep at the time. He gave it to me because he has sulfates or some such."

"That was nice."

"Old guy. Bald. Real talker. But, yeah, nice."

They drove in silence out of the maze that is a major airport these days. Cathy had learned early on that Robbie speaks in bursts. Like a hose with a kink in it, he shuts up for a while, then there's a spurt, maybe a dribble or two, followed by silence.

"Show went okay," he said suddenly. "Made some good sales the first day, not much after what. We'll see what happens the rest of the month. After that, the pieces will go into storage until we get another show out that way. No sense sending it all back here. Got plenty for that show in Oklahoma, don't you think?"

Cathy automatically agreed. The woodcarving brought in the money but, beyond that, she couldn't understand how the business worked and why people paid so much for a wooden bird.

"My ex was decent about everything. They had a party for Briana and I gave her the gift. She seemed to like it. Hard to do a portrait like that, though. And I was working off a photograph. But her husband and kids were... well... decent is the word."

"But that's it? No more child support, right?"

Robbie breathed in. "Yup. It's over."

As she maneuvered through the late night traffic on the highway, Cathy thought it might have been better if she hadn't asked that question. Robbie looked straight ahead and then said, "I'll still visit though. And she can come back here to visit."

"Who? Trisha?"

"No, that won't happen. Briana. No, Trish wouldn't come here. That's one of the reasons we broke up."

Over the years, Cathy had heard enough about the break up and Trisha and Briana, for that matter, and all the reasons the girl could go all over the country for one thing or another but never to Dallas.

Robbie looked down at his hands for quite a while as Cathy guided the sport utility van off the highway on a ramp that made the tight turn onto Frontier Avenue. About a mile down the road, she would turn onto Chandler, to the big house at the end of the block, where two boys and their older sister were stringing up a "Welcome Home" sign in the living room.

"It went fine," Robbie shrugged. "Really did."

"So what is it?"

"Well, when I first got there to the graduation, to where they were all lined up to go up the stairs and then onto the field, I saw Briana, so I went up to her. She recognized me, of course."

Robbie twitched his mouth to one side, closing his left eye. A bad sign, thought Cathy.

"And she said, 'Come to check up on your investment, Daddy?'"

Cathy slowed the pace of the van and turned into a shopping center parking lot because Robbie, for some reason, had started to cry. When she came to a complete stop, he actually sobbed a few times. She waited for him to stretch his arm toward her and when he did, she threaded hers over his shoulders.

A few moments later, back on Frontier Avenue, Cathy said, "So they're giving away wine on airplanes now?"

The cell phone alarm, the sound of rain falling in a forest, hadn't even started when I awoke at 3:30 a.m. and I couldn't remember sleeping. I must have though, because I felt fine.

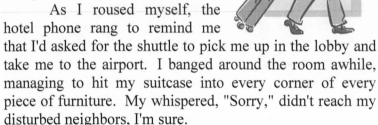

As I roused myself, the hotel phone rang to remind me that I'd asked for the shuttle to pick me up in the lobby and take me to the airport. I banged around the room awhile, managing to hit my suitcase into every corner of every piece of furniture. My whispered, "Sorry," didn't reach my disturbed neighbors, I'm sure.

For all my fumbling, I was the first person to show up for the ride. The man behind the desk lifted his hand in a greeting and when I started in his direction, signaled me that I should just wait over there, by the door, don't bother coming over here.

In the ten minutes that it took for the shuttle to arrive from the airport, for the driver to dismount, go inside, chat with the man behind the desk, go back out to the little van, come back inside the lobby and then finally ask, "Ready to go?", a couple arrived. And then a young woman. So, counting the driver, that made me "the fifth."

Somewhere I read that five is the perfect number of characters in an opera and, therefore, has been the basic set-up for theater, movies and television. Think about it. There was Ricky, Lucy, Fred and Ethel. So they had to have "a fifth." It might be a recurring character or a different one each week, like Hans Conried teaching them all better English. ("As I tippy tippy toe through my garden..." Remember?)

Anyway, if there were any high drama on the bus, I would play the role of the older gentleman, dressed in a suit, who imparts some pearl of wisdom to the married couple just before, sadly, exiting the scene, a victim of some kind.

Why the suit? Well, it's a habit now, but, at first, I had a theory. The jacket takes up a lot of room in a suitcase so, if you're going to wear some kind of coat anyway, shoulders make the perfect hanger. But then I began to suspect that the better you dress, the better you get treated.

As I reviewed the cast on the bus, I decided that the ingenue could not have any lines. Her head, covered in thick brown hair pulled back in a ponytail, never broke visual contact with her electronic device. Tiffany (I named her) gazed into its beaming face and devoted all of her attention to whatever it was showing her. Oblivious to the rest of the world, she almost had to be led to the door of the van.

The couple? The wife, maybe 40 years old, moved mechanically from station to station. From their room to the elevator. From the elevator to the lobby. From the lobby to the door. From the door to the van. The husband, however, was frantic. He frisked himself several times. He searched the outside pockets of the bags. He interrogated the wife, but she just shook her head. Even on the shuttle, he continued this constant movement. I saw a bit of myself in him and had to stop watching.

The driver would have to be the hero. Steady, competent, friendly, he whisked us off to the airport and all of us were helped out of the shuttle, our bags plopped at our sides. He smiled as I gave him a tip, but nodded slightly toward the distracted girl and the man who'd lost something. My little shake of the head was all the sympathy I could muster.

Having my passport and a boarding pass in hand, I lined up for security, which, in just a few moments, precisely at 5 a.m., would welcome me as their first customer of the day. But then I saw an alternative line, one set at a 45 degree angle. Employees, I assumed, but no, passengers too. And who should be at the head of that line? Of course, the couple from the shuttle.

And here is where the mystery was solved. Darting in front of me, the man bleated to the uniformed man behind a small podium, "I can't find my passport!"

A look that said, "It's already started," flashed across the security guy's face. "Driver's license?" he asked.

"Sure, I've got that," he almost shouted and produced one. "But what am I going to do in Miami? I can't leave the U.S. without my passport, can I?" The man in the uniform shook his head and mumbled something that, along with the wife's coaxing, moved him forward, out of my way.

Believe me, I wanted to comment on that little scene and fill in some background as well, but I have learned the most important rule in any security line. "Say as little as possible, if that."

Perhaps just to make sure everything was in working order, the security crew cut me out of the herd and gave me the benefit of their extensive training in screening passengers. "You have a dime in your pocket," the man who seemed to be in charge announced. I reached into the pocket he'd pointed at and pulled out a quarter. "You're right!" I exclaimed as if he were a magician and I a member of the audience. That threat to national security out of the way, I was allowed to proceed.

But it did occur to me that it would have been so much better if the couple had been the ones put through the x-ray machine and patted down thoroughly. Maybe then, they would have found the missing passport.

Eschew. What a remarkable word. It does sound like a sneeze, doesn't it? The "Dictionary of Word Origins," by John Ayto, reveals to me that the word began in Germany, traveled through France and ended up in English and is a relative of the word, "shy." A French variant of the word became the  English, "skew." In Spanish, to "esquivar" is to dodge or go around something. All of which adds up to eschew, "to avoid habitually especially on moral or practical grounds."

Therefore... I eschew overhead bins on airplanes.

That means I packed my main piece of luggage to be checked in at the ticket counter in Fresno to be carried off on the conveyor belt. I trust that, at my final destination, Santiago in the Dominican Republic, when the big silver carousel roars into action, my bag will be one of those coming down the chute sooner or later.

My one carry-on bag fits under the seat in front of me.

Eschewing the overhead bin changes everything, believe me. I don't have to crowd forward and try to board as soon as possible and I avoid the furious search for an open space up there. I deliberately hold back and make my entrance as late as I can so the inconvenience, both mine and my seatmates, is limited to one time.

Going back to that larger bag, the one stored in the belly of the aircraft, everything in there could be lost without regret. Those ties that I seldom wear but would never throw away, the underwear that I wouldn't want the hospital staff to see were I to be wheeled in to the emergency room, those pants that harken back to another decade and every sock that has lost its mate got placed in that bag. If I were to be standing at the mouth of the luggage carousel and that bag (also expendable) were not to emerge, I could walk away disappointed but not devastated.

Yes, this does mean that I am not the most fashionably-dressed guy in line for the tour of the rum factory, but, at my age, people generally don't look beyond the obvious: pale, bald and wears glasses. In fact, there are times when I become completely invisible to others, so the quality of my attire is not really an issue.

This is why I had a pleasant smile on my face as the flight to Miami was announced on that chilly February morning. Let the others, especially that couple I'd seen on the shuttle bus from the hotel, fidget and squirm, jockey for position, anticipating the announcement, "We are now boarding..."

I could see the man barking into his cell phone, shaking his head, heaving great sighs of frustration and then, finally, being called up to the podium. "Mr. George Stanley, please report to..." And before the last words were broadcast, George was there. A man in blue overalls, a hat and those old-fashioned large earphones clamped on his head led Mr. Stanley into the tunnel leading to the airplane.

My attention shifted to Mrs. Stanley, who watched her husband go and it did not appear she would miss him. In fact, she finally seemed at ease, completely content and I wondered if all wives, my own included, would react the same way in a similar situation.

Then came the moment. The call! "Head 'em up! Move em' out!" The herd of passengers stirred, grabbed their briefcases, carry-ons, babies, duffels, plastic bags and whatever else and formed a line. One by one, we handed over our boarding passes and were dispatched to the gangway that would take us to Florida.

Most of the chaos had subsided when I came down the aisle, seeking row 22, seat A, which I knew would be by the window. The aisle seat was empty and, in seat B, why there was Mrs. George Stanley, that serene look on her face gone, replaced by irritation. I thought my squeezing by her was the source of her displeasure and apologized for being so inconsiderate as to want to be seated all the way to the Atlantic shores.

"Oh, no problem," she said sweetly. And I saw that her attention was focused on the tarmac below, to the scene in which the ground crew tossed our luggage onto a conveyor belt. And there, in the midst of all that activity, stood Mr. George Stanley with a large suitcase spread out on the asphalt. He suddenly snapped up from the squat he'd assumed to search the contents and held up for all to see, but especially the woman in seat 22-B, a tiny blue book, a passport.

"He found it," she said to me without joy. "I tried to tell him that he didn't need a passport to go on a cruise, but it doesn't matter. He couldn't stop looking for it."

"Well now he can relax," I said.

She snorted. "You don't know my husband. All this means is that he'll have to find something else to worry about. Trust me, it will come to him by the time he gets here."

"I used to be the same way," I smiled. "Drove my wife crazy."

And without a trace of sarcasm, she said, "And now, you fly alone."

George Stanley, as predicted, had discovered a fresh source of consternation by the time he scooted down the aisle, the last to board. He took his seat on the aisle next to his wife, Eileen, and, next to the window, me.

"Bad weather in Florida," George gasped as he buckled his seat belt. "Remember we heard it on the news last night? Well, I heard from the guys on the ground," and he gestured toward the window, "that it's a pretty bad storm. I'm surprised we're getting out of here on time."

The very first rays of sunlight were trying to penetrate a blanket of clouds over the Texas plains and all appeared tranquil to me, but maybe George was right. Eileen urged him to calm down, wait and see, surely these people operating a major airline know what they're doing.

And what we were doing at that moment and for the next hour was... nothing. The sun had risen and, for a brief moment, beamed a bright light at us, but then ascended into the overcast. The captain had, by that time, given us some incomprehensible explanation for our delay. Had we really boarded all these passengers without having enough crew members on the plane?

George, tired of being ignored by his wife, directed a series of questions in my direction. I had no answers, but I did inquire about his life. "Where are you from?"

Southern California, where he and Eileen managed properties, some of them theirs, but others owned by clients, and we just had to get away this winter, although the weather there is pretty nice, but always wanted to cruise the Caribbean, so here we are.

Property management. Rental homes. Well, I had a story on that subject and it was fresh in mind. Looking back, I'm not sure I told it to the Stanley's or recalled it while we waited for that last crew member.

I had taken a court interpreting assignment and was waiting for the morning session to resume. The staff was kind enough to invite me back to a little kitchen-like area. We weren't talking about the Super Bowl, although it had been played the previous weekend, but the court clerk said she expected it would be a very busy the week after the game.

"It's the biggest day of the year for wife-beating arrests," she said.

I wanted specifics, but, before being able to slip in a few questions, the conversation careened off in another direction, problems with tenants.

"We once rented a house to a relative," the court reporter said. "Worst mistake we ever made. Besides the usual problems, not paying the rent on time, running down the place, the thing that bothered me most was that, when they finally did move out, they took every light bulb with them. You're not going to believe this, but they even took the one in the refrigerator."

That prompted a second clerk, the lady who knew the secret of the Super Bowl, to tell her story.

"We rented a house out for a brief time. I remember it was winter because I was wearing a coat. I knocked on the house of the little rental and the wife answered. She seemed awfully nervous. I asked her for the rent and she said, 'Come in.'"

"She had never asked me to come in before. I was reluctant and told her I had to take my daughter to school. Her husband was standing in the hallway. I could see him there. When I asked the wife about the rent again, she looked at him and he said, 'Tomorrow.' So the wife turned back to me and said, 'We'll have it for you tomorrow. Come back tomorrow.'"

"That night, on the television news, we saw our rental home. Sometime between noon and 1 p.m., that man had taken a hammer and beat the woman to death. We found out later that he'd come back unexpectedly from a job interview in Southern California and found her packed up and ready to leave him."

"That's why she wanted you to go inside," the court reporter gasped and the storyteller lowered her eyes.

"You would have been killed too," the other clerk interjected.

"I've thought about that," she continued. "I told my husband that night to sell the house. I didn't want to rent it to anyone anymore. We sold it right away."

"Well folks," the friendly voice broke in, "this is the captain and it appears the flight bringing our crew member from Florida has been delayed. In fact, the plane he's on can't take off because of bad weather so we can either wait here so we don't lose our place in line or... uh... let you folks wait in more comfortable surroundings. Actually, it's better we weren't out there on the taxiway because we wouldn't have a choice. Anyway, we're checking to see how long it will take to get a different crew member here so we can be on our way to Miami. Thank you for your patience."

There are a few ways to spend time during a flight delay. No need to list them here. What I did was think back to another time and another island. Hawaii in 2006.

3

Aloha To You Too

My bags for the trip to the Dominican Republic were packed just the way Anna would do it.

She's quite an expert at this and is willing to invest the time it takes to do it right. When we went to Hawaii in 2006, for example, the actual packing started at 1:30 a.m. and we had to get to the Fresno Yosemite International Airport by 5 a.m. But cutting it close is part of her method.

"I learned it from my father," she told me once. "He was the master at this. He could pack an entire house into a small box." Anna turned out to be a good student. She filled from the center, cushioning the corners and made sure the load was balanced.

I have been amazed over and over when what appears to be an incredible mountain of clothing, gifts and food dwindles as she transfers all of it into a few pieces of luggage. She weighed our load that particular morning before heading for the airport and, believe it or not, each suitcase came within an ounce or two of the maximum allowed.

We arrived at the airport at 4:30 a.m. and the security line was open and moving. We checked in and got our boarding passes, waved good bye to our daughter Anisa and started walking down the long corridor to the very end of the terminal to catch our plane to Los Angeles.

It appears to be a hard and fast rule. Whenever the Watrous' take a flight, the gate must be as far away from the entrance as possible. At Los Angeles International, we had time for a big cup of coffee before being herded into the freight cars. Well, boarded the plane.

We had called home and found out that our automatic sprinklers were going crazy. No matter what our adult daughter did, they wouldn't stop squirting water all over the lawn, which was completely soaked at that point. It reminded me of the old Disney movie, "Fantasia," the one where the mops and buckets just keep popping up. The water was rising and Anisa sounded as if she was getting ready to bail.

Speaking of bail, Anna's pre-trip preparations consisted of looking up the address of DaKine Bail Bonds, the one owned by the guy known as "Dog the Bounty Hunter" Chapman. "Man, I guess we're going to have a better time than I expected," I laughed when she told me about it.

She printed out maps to the office on Queen Emma St. and they were somewhere in all that luggage so we could pay the Chapman's a visit, maybe swap stories about going to court.

The sprinkler situation was solved by a neighbor but not until the estate was completely encircled by a moat. But we were able to relax on board the jet bound for Honolulu for five and a half hours.

The people around us were interesting. A couple and the husband's dad were going to Hawaii as a 90th birthday gift. The old guy had been stationed at Pearl Harbor during the war and hadn't been back since then. After watching them a while, I decided that the two of them had been estranged for quite a while and they had just reconciled. All conjecture, of course, but it made the time pass.

The movie, "Take the Lead," was almost as entertaining. Antonio Banderas played a French school teacher who reforms his worst students by inviting them to learn ballroom dancing instead of vandalizing cars. There's the competition at the end and everyone goes home happy and a bit wiser.

We saw the veteran, his son and daughter-in-law later on at the Alamo Rental place. Maybe they would have liked the electric blue mini-SUV but Anna got to it first. We gave them a friendly wave as we pulled away from the curb and headed toward the New Otani Hotel.

Perhaps you have heard that tourists like us can eschew a rental car and just take "The Bus" around the island for an excitingly small amount of money. Not true. This wasn't our first trip to Hawaii. We made the trip a few years before with some friends, one of whom decided to assume the role of tour guide. After checking into a cozy, centrally-located hotel just a couple of blocks from the ocean, we set out to find a place to eat.

We watched the waves at Waikiki for a few moments and then wandered down the street when we saw a bus. We chased it down just outside of Kapiolani Park, jumped on, laughed as we all dutifully dropped our quarters in the box and found the few empty seats available. The driver gave us a look, but didn't say anything, just put it in gear, lurched ahead about 200 yards and pulled up.

"Last stop!" he sang. "Everyone out!"

So we walked and, as the sun set slowly in the west and the island was gradually plunged into darkness, we trudged along until Amanda, my younger daughter, who couldn't have been even a teenager yet, asked me a question.

"What's X X X mean? And why does it say, 'Girls! Girls! Girls!'? Aren't boys allowed?" She waited for me to turn red and start to explain before bursting into raucous laughter.

So we ended up calling a taxi, which was, as we used to say, "A trip." Amanda and I sat in the very back because we don't get car sick by driving north while looking south like others in our party.

After driving around for a while, we spotted the perfect restaurant. As we all sat there, congratulating ourselves on finding this jewel and studying its fascinating menu, I looked across the street and saw our hotel.

And so convenient too!

When we opened the door to our room on the eighth floor of the New Otani Hotel the early afternoon of July 4, 2006, we discovered a large closet, a bed and a sliding glass door and no room for anything else.

Our first mistake was leaving both doors open as we tried to haul in our luggage. A blast of the trade winds, strong enough to propel a sailing ship back to the mainland, lifted up everything weighing less than two pounds and ushered it toward the balcony or lanai, as it's called in Hawaii.

After scampering around to save our possessions, we shut the door to the hallway and walked out on the lanai and looked up at Diamond Head, that famous crag named by British sailors. The story I heard was that they looked up at the impressive sight, thought they saw something glittering and immediately ran up there to find diamonds. There weren't any, but the name stuck.

Our room overlooked Kapiolani Park, which I assume was named for the Hawaiian princess who defied the fire goddess Pele in December of 1824. According to historians, she mocked the missionaries at first by walking into their houses completely naked to ask some impertinent question about religion. But, somewhere along the way, the princess started to respond to their message and, after putting on a new change of clothes, set out from Hilo on the Big Island with a hundred brave souls, all determined to bear witness to the Christian god. After working their way through the tropical forest and then up through the lava flows, Kapiolani and her entourage reached Kilauea and looked into the huge volcano Mauna Loa.

With Joseph Goodrich of the Hilo mission at her side, the princess announced that, the next day, she would go to the volcano and prove Pele was not to be feared. Although they'd walked with her a hundred miles, some of the group tried to convince her that the wise course would be to worship this new god brought by missionaries from New England but without offending the old gods.

The next day, Kapiolani started out by eating a whole branch of berries rather than offering half to Pele, which, in itself, should have resulted in her death. Then, just to seal her fate, she uttered the words that were immortalized in poetry by Alfred Lord Tennyson.

"Jehovah is my god," she shouted down at the volcano. "I fear not Pele. Should I perish by her anger, then you may fear her powers. But if Jehovah saves me, then you must fear and serve Jehovah." She walked away without a scratch and lived for 17 years after that demonstration of faith.

From our lanai at the New Otani, we could see the ocean if we peeked around another large building. It was an impressive sight but the wind was howling and we decided to retreat. If we wanted to get a better look at the beach, then Anna and I would have to go downstairs and out the door, which we planned on doing, but first we had to set out to explore Waikiki.

The guide book said the Tony Roma Restaurant was only ten minutes away and those ribs sounded pretty good so off we went.

Our rental car, an SUV, carried us out of the parking garage at the New Otani Hotel to Kapiolani Park, but then things got complicated. The two-way street becomes a one-way at some point and then there's the Ali Wai Canal, but, whoa, was that McCully? We should have turned there, but let's go around and give it another try.

The rib place had thoughtfully put up a big sign so I could see it and we pulled into the parking lot on our second or third pass. We were led to a table and seated next to a couple of women a bit older than ourselves who had been slugging down rum drinks and complaining about their kids for a while. They didn't lower their voices or change the subject just because a couple had been placed virtually at their respective elbows.

We ordered, tried not to be too upset that Doris' boy Freddie had decided to quit college right in the middle of the semester without telling her or that Grace, the youngest of Alice's girls, was separating from her husband of only two years. The ribs arrived and we immersed ourselves in the aroma and the fun of putting barbecue meat in our empty bellies. We were thus occupied when the ladies left and took their troubles with them. I almost said, "Tell Freddie and Grace I said hello," but held back.

After dinner, we walked down this wide avenue and ran right into the ABC Store, the first of many we were to visit over the next week. It's quite a place. They have a sandal there that is perfection. We should have picked up a dozen pairs, but were unaware of their unique beauty. There is something about the construction that provides its wearer with the utmost in comfort and, in the bargain, a satisfying squeak with every step you take.

It was there that I replenished my supply of Hawaii post cards. I'd taken ones bought previously on the airplane when we left Fresno earlier that day and started writing messages like, "Getting a good tan here on Waikiki and Anna has learned the hula and how to play drums." Turn the card over and you'd see the beach and a hula dancer with a conga drum player in the background. Pretty clever, eh? The trouble was I didn't think to get stamps so these cards still wouldn't get in the mail until the next day. It's a race to see who gets back first, me or the cards.

As we walked back to our car, we stopped and gazed at an entire wall of water. A hotel had placed an aquarium right there next to the street. It was enormous and entertaining with fish darting around inside. I couldn't resist. "Lookee big fishee!" I cried out and got a chuckle from Anna. People walking by jumped, shook their heads and stayed out of our way.

Everything seemed so perfect but then I drove the SUV out of the parking lot and, for the next 48 minutes, made one wrong turn after another. Meanwhile, overhead, the fireworks were launched from two different sources, the Schofield Barracks near the very center of the island of Oahu and Bayfest farther up the coast on the windward side.

As we climbed up one road and then another, miles off course, fireworks burst right over our heads. Then we ran into a battalion of firemen out extinguishing one of the 78 fires that would be ignited that night. We found that out from the newspaper the next day and thought it was pretty serious, but the reporter added that this was 25 fewer than the year before.

But the fire we saw turned out to be, in its own crazy way, the key to our success in finding our hotel. The firemen turned us around and pointed us back toward Honolulu. I had driven Anna far past Diamond Head and we were headed for parts unknown. Eventually, we made it all the way back to Tony Roma's and, from there, back to the New Otani.

As we took refuge in our room on the eighth floor, I pulled open the drapes and discovered a full moon beaming down at us. We had braved the night in Honolulu, dodged the fireworks, wandered around in the dark and were safe once again.

After our first night, we awoke to the sound of a gentle breeze. The gale force winds had died down overnight, but that meant rain-laden clouds could now float up over the Pali (the cliffs) and dump showers on the east side of Oahu. Still, the temperatures were supposed to stay under 90.

We opened the door to our room at the New Otani on Queen's Beach on Waikiki and found a copy of the Honolulu Advertiser for July 5, 2006. The newspaper announced that it had been in operation for 150 years and that the North Koreans had just fired off a missile that proved U.S. soil was within reach of their weapons. And it also reported that the Space Shuttle Discovery was in orbit and would be tracked by a station on the islands.

All well and good but where was that Maui Divers van that was supposed to pick us up for our free breakfast and orientation tour? We were counting on their guidance to get us to Hilo Hattie's where souvenirs were waiting. But none of this was happening and, by our internal clock, it was getting close to noon and we were hungry.

I checked with the bell captain and the parking valet. They both said the same thing. "Oh, they come by here every day and drive people around trying to sell them tour packages. Believe me, you're better off without it. Big waste of time."

But if we took off on our own in our rental car, which had a full tank of gas and sun roof, we would be placing our full trust in Jim Watrous to find our way around Honolulu. But it seemed we had no choice, so we boarded the mini-SUV and then, the idiot behind the wheel told his wife, "I've been here before you know and I remember a coffee shop right in the middle of Waikiki. Let's see if I can find it."

Halfway down Ali Wai Blvd., we both realized, without a word spoken, that I wasn't going to find that place. Instead, I suggested that we head toward Honolulu, farther inland and take sustenance at the Aloha Tower Marketplace, which I recalled as an enormous place overflowing with shops, restaurants and parking.

The Ali Wai Canal serves as the border of Waikiki, but it is also the reason the place even exists. The water in the canal is drainage. The area that is now the home of all these hotels was once a swamp until some genius came up with the idea of clearing the area, bringing in sand from other islands and creating one of the most famous spots on earth. Before that, only a couple of strips of beach existed, such as the one in front of the New Otani, and those were for the exclusive use of royalty.

As interesting as that might have been, I knew better than to bring it up at that moment. I needed to invest all my energy and intelligence in getting down the road to the Aloha Tower. Finally, I saw boats, the kind Gilligan and the Skipper take on a three-hour tour, then a gigantic clock tower.

Back in the glory days of the cruise ships, this was the anchorage. The newspapers would announce "a boat day" and the arrival of these huge floating gold mines. Merchants, missionaries and pretty girls would all be there to greet the passengers and crew. Even the "Merry Monarch," the king himself, Charles Kalakaua would entertain visitors in his boathouse and throw back a few drinks.

Writers Mark Twain and Robert Louis Stevenson vouched for this portly king as a most hospitable host who treated everyone else like royalty and didn't spare any expense on himself either.

Unfortunately, his highness had long since departed this paradise and, as a matter of fact, even though it was 9 a.m., it appeared that everyone else had too. We seemed to be almost entirely alone. The click of our ABC sandals on the tile floor created an eerie echo. Was this an episode of Twilight Zone? Had we slept through some mass evacuation of coastal Honolulu? Were the people who usually thronged to the marketplace at this moment on space ships manned by creatures reading a book called, "To Serve Man"?

No, it was just early by island standards. But there was a food court upstairs, just around a turn and up the elevator, which was not working at the moment. Anna leaned against an uncooperative escalator, whose stairs were apparently at rest, waiting for some maintenance man to flip a switch.

"I'm not taking another step," she announced.

In spite of her protest to the contrary, Anna did climb the escalator to the food court at the Aloha Tower because, otherwise, they would not have known how she wanted her eggs cooked. We were served two breakfast specials and tried to read each other's mind.

After eating there at the food court at Aloha Tower, we appeared to be on a quest, one in which I was neither taking the lead, nor being informed of the objective. A counter with the attractive sign, "Bad Ass Coffee" drew our attention and, after chatting with the young lady there, we continued on our way with a bag of our first purchases to be taken home and distributed as gifts to those who hadn't been able to accompany us.

It was on the tip of my tongue to suggest that we visit the Hawaii Maritime Museum, which I realized was right next door, or maybe go up the Aloha Tower and get a panoramic view of the island when Anna suddenly veered off into a Starbuck's. She came out in a few moments and walked directly to the Nail Shop which was conveniently just around a corner. After a quick consultation, she came back to tell me, "This is going to take about an hour."

Well, I guess I can wander around on my own. My bride disappeared into the luxury that is a nail and massage spa while I stood forlorn, clutching a bag with "Bad Ass Coffee" mugs inside.

Alone in Honolulu again. In November of 2002, I ventured off on my own, an impulsive decision, one I immediately regretted. As a matter of fact, I had fully intended on Anna's company on that trip.

The whole idea was for me to take her to the travel agency in Madera and, in the middle of arranging this solo excursion, suddenly turn to her and say, "Why don't you come with me?" Her eyes would grow wide and she would ask, "Do you mean it?" Of course I did and then the agent would produce the paperwork to make it all a reality.

But she declined. We were, in those days, the contracted agency to provide interpreting services for Madera County's courts and we had just come back from a wedding in New York City. I thought we could let the operation run itself for another week, but my partner in the business wasn't so sure.

Who knows what motivated me to say, at that moment, "All right then. I'll just go by myself." But I did. And it was a bargain. A new, small hotel in the middle of

Waikiki was opening and it had basically thrown open its doors to tourists just to catch the public's eye. It caught mine. "The Bamboo" would host me practically for free if I would just take this very inexpensive flight to and from Oahu.

I had a small, blue notebook filled with ideas on how to get around Honolulu in trolleys and buses as well as trips and excursions like the Royal Circle Island Tour, the Paradise Cove Luau among others. From the very beginning, things did not go as planned. The day my week in Honolulu was to start, fog settled in at the Fresno Air Terminal and my flight to San Francisco was delayed for hours.

From the time the wheels go up to the time they touch down, the entire trip only takes 35 minutes, but the 6:35 a.m. flight was canceled entirely due to the lack of visibility. At first, the mood at Gate 8 was calm, unperturbed, but that would change as the view out the window remained the same. Telephones were being pulled out of pockets and purses. Voices ranged from mutters to loud complaints, but an older man and I, both traveling alone, weren't that upset.

We engaged in conversation and I found out he was born in Arkansas about 70 years ago but had lived most of his adult life in Strathmore, a little town south of Fresno.

"I was married for 35 years and then my wife died," he said. "But a man isn't meant to be alone. So I decided last night to take this trip. Maybe find me an Ozark woman on vacation. Dumb but easy to live with."

He smelled of cigarettes and I could tell he wanted one at that moment, but airports don't tolerate that anymore. "I smoke because I like it," he said. "If it wasn't so far to walk, I'd go all the way back to the entrance and fire one up. But I don't have that kind of energy anymore."

I thought of saying, "It's the cigarettes," but I didn't.

"I wouldn't normally go alone on a trip," he said. "You gotta' have someone with you or it's no good," and he mentioned the "Ozark woman" again.

"I've been out that way before," he said, nodding toward the windows and the fog but meaning the Pacific. "During the war. Even went to Tokyo on leave. Nothing but bars and whorehouses back then."

We passed the time until 8:35 when the fog, which actually got worse for a while, lifted enough for us to be summoned to the gate. "Well," he said, "see you in Hawaii." He stuck out a gnarled, purple hand and I shook it.

We took our places in the airplane and for about a half an hour, I gave that older man and his life some deep thought until it occurred to me that we had not moved. The fog had returned.

As I waited for my wife to finish getting her nails done, the Aloha Tower Marketplace started to fill up with tourists. None of them were alone. In fact, they seemed to be organized into groups of at least five.

I sat at a table and watched them take turns buying tea and coffee, maybe a pastry, and then settling in for almost exactly ten minutes. Then, as if it were all rehearsed, one group would pick up and leave and another one would take its place. Oh, and they were all Japanese. It dawned on me later on that perhaps there was a tour bus parked outside and they had all streamed out of it and would stream back on a precise schedule.

Out of consideration, I removed myself from the table and sat on a ledge so that I might better observe the proceedings. Also, from that vantage point, I could keep an eye on the Nail Shop and, in the bargain, people would get the impression (the correct one) that I was a husband in waiting and not alone in Honolulu.

At one point, I walked to the Starbucks and got a dose of caffeine and, on my return to the corner of the ledge, was halted by a bug. It was a cockroach about the size of a small mouse and it was pale yellow.

I had with me one of the best guidebooks I have ever read entitled, "Oahu Revealed" and it had a page dedicated to this subject. There weren't even mosquitoes in Hawaii at all until the good ship Wellington dumped bilge water into a stream in Maui in 1826, but even so the constant trade winds seem to keep them away from areas most frequented by tourists. But spiders and centipedes are a different story.

According to the authors, these bugs can grow to a size of six inches in length and are very aggressive. A sting from one of them, even a baby, can cause pain ranging from what a bee inflicts up to what you feel when a kid fires a pellet into you with his BB rifle. The book added that some island doctors prescribed staying drunk for three days while the agony subsides.

I had stopped in the middle of the courtyard at Aloha Tower with one hand holding a cup of coffee and the other my guidebook. I glanced down at the bug at my foot as I read and then, just to be on the safe side, squashed the critter.

The constant rotation of tourists at the tables was not interrupted by this preemptive strike and none of them seemed to care that I left the carcass right there where I'd committed the deed.

Maybe I've got a little Billy in me.

My younger brother, from an early age, demonstrated an interest and aptitude for agriculture, the growing of crops, the raising of animals and the killing of bugs that infest both. When Anna and I were first married and returned to Madera from New York City, it was Billy who provided us with our first car.

It was a Volkswagen Beetle (coincidence?) which had lost its front bumper somewhere. Billy had installed a wooden block in its place. The little car had been through the fields continuously as my younger brother plied his trade, "field checker" for the Melville E. Wilson Co. As I understand it, he would ride into the furrows or the groves, take up a position with a net and capture whatever was flying around. Other times, he would collect what had been caught in traps hanging from the branches or vines. After analyzing his finds, he could recommend which pesticide or insecticide to apply.

At any rate, Billy moved on from there and began killing other pests as well. And he didn't just have bugs in his sights either. Billy became famous for tracking down mice and disposing of them. And he had flair too. Once, there was apparently some discussion at a staff meeting at this one extermination service that employed him about the need to document the number of mice removed.

This was probably one of those situations where a manager makes a general statement but actually is directing it to only one person. And, in this case, that person would be Billy because no one killed as many mice as he did. In fact, I'd venture to say that he was so busy poisoning and disposing of them he couldn't keep track of the number.

But he didn't raise his hand or complain, just nodded and went on his way to the next job. The next day, however, when the office staff went out to their cars at the end of the day, each of them found a mouse impaled on their aerials. The story I heard was that, when confronted by the manager on this point, Billy said, "I had enough for two or three for each car but I couldn't bring myself to slide them down far enough to make that happen."

Wasps were another of Billy's particular favorites. The majority of pest control people just don't like dealing with wasps. They can be dangerous and, like rodents, hard to find. A nest of them can be almost anywhere.

There was a warehouse type store in Fresno that had a problem with wasps flying around, bothering the customers and workers, so the call went out and Billy was the one chosen to respond.

He told his assistant to mount two tanks on his back and hand him a wand for each hand. Then Billy marched into the store and began picking off stray wasps. Up and down the aisles he went, firing with his right hand and his left, dropping the unsuspecting flying creatures like, well, like flies.

The store manager came running. "What are you doing?" he screamed. Billy just smiled. "Killing wasps. That's what you wanted, right?"

But not this way, the man raged. The customers had cleared the aisles and were huddled in the relative safety of the check-out lanes. The manager pointed at them. "You're scaring people."

And then he suggested, "getting to the root of the problem."

A light went on in my brother's brain. "Oh yeah, the root of the problem," he repeated. "Good idea."

So he went back out to the truck and told his assistant, "Suit me up. All the way. Radio it in." As instructed, he helped Billy into the complete hazardous material outfit, helmet, mask, tanks and then advised dispatch, "Billy is going in."

The white-suited Watrous strode into the store again and people scattered. The manager approached and heard a muffled, "The roof? How do I get to the roof?"

He must have pointed in the right direction because Billy was soon on the roof, going from spot to spot until he came upon an air conditioning unit. Turning toward the assistant, who was on the radio with dispatch, he pointed with the wand and commenced the attack.

The assistant reported that the enemy had been engaged. Billy began pouring it on. He had the wasps at his mercy. They never expected this kind of furious offensive. Confused, the wasps retreated.

Customers and workers began pouring out of of the front doors. Some walked quickly, others ran. The wasps had been forced down into the store to get away from the monster that had sneaked up on them from the rear. The assistant told dispatch all about this and then, off in the distance, he heard a siren.

"The fire department's showed up," he shouted. "Is there a fire?"

"No, there's no fire. There's a million wasps in that store. Tell Billy. Abort! Abort! Whatever he's doing, tell him to stop doing it!"

The assistant passed on the information and Billy got the message. Without a word, he laid down the wand, took off the white hazmat suit and, in a few minutes, casually walked out the front door of the store as the firemen were rushing in.

He got in the passenger side of the pest control truck and told the assistant, "We'll come back later for the stuff. Drive, man, drive."

His legend grew and Billy never had any trouble getting pest control jobs. Nor did he get any lip about filling out forms again. Maybe it seems strange, but there is some satisfaction in ridding the planet of a pest. I felt it myself as I walked away from that poisonous bug at the Aloha Tower Marketplace.

After my confrontation with a bug, I again took a spot on the ledge near the nail salon where my wife was receiving ablutions and ministrations. My telephone vibrated and I answered. It was Anna, who advised me of the  progress being made and estimated that the staff would complete their work in about 20 minutes.

"Find a place to have lunch. Think you can do that?" See, she was coming around.

I didn't have to search far. Don Ho, the famous Hawaiian singer, had a restaurant right there in that same complex and what a rave review it received in my guide book, "Oahu Revealed."

"The restaurant is on the water overlooking the industrial but nonetheless peaceful Honolulu Harbor. And it really is relaxing to see giant container ships passing by. Thatched roofs add an exotic touch."

At first, I worried that we'd get there before it opened but, as the minutes past, I realized that fear was unfounded. Anna called again and said, "Break a $20 into four five's and come by." I did as I was told and was allowed into that world of manicure, pedicure and other operations foreign to me. The staff knew who I was from my wife's description and they led me back to a torture chamber where hot wax was being applied to a leg.

I recognized it immediately. "Anna?" I asked. From her face-down position, she acknowledged her identity and I handed her the bills, hoping that they would set her free without inflicting much more pain. About ten minutes later, my wife emerged with a smile. Her nails, all twenty, must have felt wonderful and her legs seemed to be in working order, so we walked over to Don Ho's place, where a waitress immediately seated us at a table overlooking the harbor and a Japanese container ship.

In fact, the crew had lined up to disembark. They were children, just boys and girls, maybe 13 years old at the most. At least, that's how it appeared. I thought it was some kind of school at sea program. Surely, these were not the toughened sailors you expect to find on the bounding main or down at the docks.

How about a drink? The waitress directed my attention from the kiddie crew filing off the vessel to a list of libations. I got a pair of smiles, one from the waitress and the other from Anna, when I selected a "Beach Monkey" drink.

"And do you want to take the monkey with you?" I shrugged because I'd heard that joke before but where was the part about the woman with the ugly baby on the bus? "I love asking that question," the girl added. There was an uncomfortable pause. "Well, do you want the monkey or not?" That's when I realized that the coconut is supposed to look like a monkey's head and I felt it only right to say I'd take one.

Anna laughed and the skies cleared. I could stop sulking and worrying about how the rest of the week would go. It would turn out to be one of the best of our travels together.

We both recalled our first anniversary, the one we celebrated by going to a swanky place on Belmont Avenue in Fresno. It's gone, of course, a victim of the fickle public and shifting population centers. Anyway, the waitress back then asked me if I wanted a martini. Caught off guard, I said yes. "Up?" she inquired. I shrugged and said yes. In a few moments, I had a glass of kerosene in front of me. Anna shook her head. "If you didn't know what she meant, why did you say yes?" For the adventure of it I guess.

We ate our lunch and drank a banana-flavored juice out of the monkey's skull. Anna suggested we go back to the New Otani so that she could submit to a lomi-lomi, which would take about an hour. Quickly, I thumbed through the guidebook and discovered that was a massage. Apparently, there had been some girl talk back at the nail salon.

Meanwhile, I got into my new bathing suit and walked along San Souci Beach, which is French for "without a care," which described my mood exactly. The sun sat in the sky about halfway between the surf and the horizon and the tourists were baking in its warmth. Although I'd never been there before, the whole scene looked very familiar.

Of course, this was the same area where that Chinese girl was drugged and then left out in the sun since dawn. Her rescuers didn't find her until late in the afternoon, but, after being hospitalized, she had a full recovery. She was an art dealer and a priceless vase was involved somehow. She would have died of exposure if Magnum PI hadn't figured it all out.

The insistent vibrating brought me back to the real world. Having been lomi-lomi'd to a sufficient degree, my bride would be joining me for a walk along the beach and then dinner at Duke's.

We strolled along the beach at Waikiki, just the two of us, and sat on the groin. No, that's not dirty talk. For some reason, the pier made of stones that sits between the Natatorium and the Diamond Head Canoe Club is called a groin. Its purpose it to keep the long currents from causing too strong a rip tide.

As we watched the wonders of Waikiki, two groups of girls were pushing their respective outrigger canoes into the water. The teams started off pretty close to one another, but then one, paddling furiously, pulled ahead of the other and kept adding to its lead. We didn't know it at the time, but they were preparing for a regatta at the end of the week.

We dressed up back in our room at the New Otani and then headed down the road to Duke's, a Hawaiian institution. True, we had to wait for a table, even on a Wednesday, but we knew it was worth it. While waiting for our table in a semi-bar atmosphere, we watched three people huddled over a table. Just from the way they dealt with each other, it was obvious one of the men and the lone woman were a couple, either married or at least in some kind of committed relationship. The second man, a bit older, was trying to convince them to do something.

The single man bought them all a round of drinks and then he said, loud enough for us to hear, that he would give them a moment to "think it over" and he retreated to a bar stool. The couple put their heads together, whispering, pondering and finally, beckoned the man to return.

Since the couple was young and attractive to some degree, my suspicion was that we were watching some kind of tawdry assignation or at least the invitation to become involved in what you might call a "romantic adventure."

Over time and having had the "benefit" of having experienced a moment something like the one we witnessed at Duke's, I'm pretty sure the older man was trying to get them to attend a time-share event, a luau perhaps, followed by a "presentation," and then the hard sell to get them to invest in a condominium.

We'll never know, of course, because the three of them suddenly scurried out of Duke's and out of our lives.

It turned out that Anna and I were visiting Duke's on the anniversary of the famous swimmer's record-breaking performance in the 1913 world championships.

Duke Kahanamku, born in 1890, lived in Wakiki until he died in 1968. He won six Olympic gold medals in swimming and water polo and had a major role in making surfing popular worldwide. When reporters arrived to interview him about his triumphs, they found Duke gliding over the waves on a long board. The photographs and stories written about Duke and Waikiki and the other boys along the beach gave birth to the surfing craze, which shows no sign of ever disappearing.

Anna ordered the chicken and I chose the steak. At some point, she got up from the table and took some video of the place. So absorbed in the meat on my plate, I lost track of her until someone knocked on the window above me. I looked up to find a camera trained on my face, which was completely engaged in chewing. It was Anna. I gave her a goofy look, no real stretch really, and waved her to come back inside.

We tumbled out of bed to find that Oahu had been busy all night preparing a golden sunrise and a soft breeze. The Hau Tree Lanai lived up to its billing and sat us down to a gourmet breakfast accompanied by the sound of the Sans Souci Beach coming to life ever so gradually.

We agreed to get a picnic lunch together and find a beach, no particular one, just one that had swaying palm trees, a little foam in the surf, a picnic table and maybe a few less people than Waikiki. Foodland Market would be our first stop and, with the directions from the front desk, it did not elude us for long. From there, we headed toward the water. We passed Sea Life Park and Makapuu Lighthouse and then a beach called Waimanalo opened up before us.

There was the table, palm trees, foam in the surf, everything we'd been looking for. To be honest, there are maybe a thousand more beaches that fit our description but this was the one we found. Of course, it was windy and we had to weigh everything down, but it was a small price to pay for paradise. We made our sandwiches and then ate them. Then we posed for pictures and video. Under a tree. In front of the beach. See the islands off shore? With the mountains behind us.

We were reluctant to leave our table unguarded because Anna likes to have everything at her fingertips. We had a large bag, too big to stow in the overhead compartment on an airplane, a brand new ice chest and many other items on display. In the midst of it all sat Anna, waving at me as I tiptoed into the water. Pretty soon, I was doing my best imitation of someone swimming when, all of sudden, there she was at my side.

"Those folks said they needed a table for a little while," she explained, indicating a group in "formal" Hawaiian wear. We stood in the water, moved around a little bit, shuffling in the sand and waves and felt about 20 years younger. The people at the table had just come from a funeral service and had gathered around to talk and eat a few snacks and maybe cry a little. They all managed to fit in a van that waited for them up on the road and waved to us as they left.

Once we'd done the same and began driving along the ocean, I spotted a familiar sight. If you will pardon me this reference, it was "Robin's Nest," the home base of Magnum PI. I recognized the gates and realized that they used practically the entire neighborhood as part of the "estate" to make it look as big as it did on television.

We passed the blow hole, where the ocean funnels into a rock and then shoots the surf into the air like a geyser. Nearby is the small beach tucked into a cliff where the famous "From Here to Eternity" scene was shot with Burt Lancaster and Deborah Kerr. People had climbed down from rocks into the cove and were paddling around in the water. We had pulled over and, from our spot, Anna caught sight of a sea turtle. When she pointed it out, everyone nearby oohed and ahhed.

As the afternoon sun started bearing down on us, we decided to make our way back to Honolulu, which made it possible for us to experience rush hour traffic. Things went much better than expected and we even spotted the post office on Saratoga Avenue near the Hawaiian Hilton. For dinner, we decided a pizza would be welcome and there was the Big Kahuna Center ready to put one together for us. After eating almost every bite of it, we hit the International Marketplace, which is supposed to be remodeled but the merchants have decided to wait until after the tourist season. The joke is, tourist season never ends.

We didn't get back the New Otani until way after sunset but, as far as I was concerned, there wasn't a postcard in my growing collection that showed a picture more beautiful than Anna, across the table, as we ate a pizza at the Big Kahuna.

Our original destination on Friday, July 7, 2006 was Hanauma Bay, which the guidebook promised would be one of the best bargains on Oahu. There's a protected body of water with lots of fish, so tame they will gather around your legs and keep you company all day if  you want. But, the authors of "Oahu Revealed" warn you to get there early.

We didn't. By the time we got our breakfast out of a fast-food drive-up window and then maneuvered around Diamond Head to the Windward Shore, the parking lots at the bay had filled to capacity. We took a long, sad look at the signs, "Parking Lot Closed," and decided to continue north.

How about the Polynesian Cultural Center? Only an hour away, it said in the book. Sun roof open, wind blowing Anna's hair, the ocean off to our right, we breezed long. We could see the hang gliders and individual sail boats at Sandy Beach and then we spotted Waimanalo Beach, where we'd had our picnic the day before.

The cliffs of the Ko'olau Range loomed over us on the driver's side. The guidebook confirmed what I was thinking. They do look higher than they actually are. Because they are sheer cliffs, it's almost as if someone had constructed a movie set for our benefit.

What we should have done was driven toward those cliffs and thereby merge on to the principal northbound highway, but, instead we hugged the coastline. We entered the town of Kailua, a wonderful place to stay while on

Oahu by all accounts, but not the easiest place to drive through. The streets are a maze of names and numbers that appear to have been designed with the intention of confusing visitors.

Stubbornly sticking to the shore, we eventually left Kailua behind and the appearance of Chinaman's Hat, an uninhabited island shaped just as you'd expect, convinced us that we were going in the right direction. From there, it was smooth driving all the way to La'ie, home of the P.C.C.

We couldn't have timed our arrival better. The place was just opening. We took a canoe ride, watched a movie about coral reefs on the IMAX screen, saw the "Parade of Canoes" in the giant lagoon and then visited each of the "islands" represented in the park. We even stayed for the buffet dinner and show. We invested seven hours and about $20 in the Polynesian Cultural Center and came away satisfied.

Back in our room at the New Otani, I thumbed through the guidebook, realizing that we wouldn't be seeing all the sights I'd planned. We wouldn't be taking in the Tiki Bar I'd discovered in its pages, nor the Round Top Drive, which had become entirely too dangerous. Even taxis were avoiding the place. An older couple had been shot and killed up there on Thursday night by a man described in the newspapers as "a 23-year-old incapacitated by mental disorders." He was the grandson of "a Waikiki developer" and his family had a restraining order against him, so he picked on someone else, this innocent couple from Los Angeles, out to visit their daughter.

But, as Anna began reshuffling the luggage, making room for all the souvenirs we'd be buying the next day, I realized that I was already seeing the sight I most came to see, her smile.

It was Saturday on the beach at Waikiki and I leaned against a low brick wall at 5:50 a.m. to watch a very coy sunrise, not over Diamond Head, but that little dip in the Ko'olau's over Kapiolani Park, which had been wiped clean overnight, except for some early morning joggers and a couple sleeping under a blanket.

The canoe clubs were out early for practice and bicyclists were streaming into the park between the New Otani and the Natatorium to begin some kind of race. As I looked out over the Sans Souci, a man to my left plucked out random tunes on his guitar and a man to my right sipped coffee and studied the beach.

A girl in a black bathing suit walked past us, snapped a white cap over her head and adjusted her goggles to her face. She plunged into the water. All business. Then there was the guy who stood up in a kayak, scooting back and forth across the water.

"He's practicing," the coffee drinker explained in that distinctive island inflection.

"Practicing what?" I asked. "Do they have races where people stand up in kayaks?"

"It's not exactly a kayak," he said.

We watched the unusual sight that developed, a man who seemed to be standing up in the water waiting for the serious swimmer to reappear. When she did, we both nodded, because going into the water by yourself didn't seem very prudent.

I went back to our room as Anna finished packing up a shipment of goodies she'd collected thus far. My participation in this job would be to contact the bell captain, get a big box and bring it back to her. I got two boxes.

That afternoon, after a quick trip to the post office, we were served lunch at the Hau Tree Lanai and then we had a front row seat on the beach scene. Families had moved in and that sent the body builders and bikini types toward the center of Waikiki. Encouraged, we finished eating, returned to our room and donned our swimming outfits.

We didn't actually swim or even stand in the water but sat right at the edge of the ocean and then let the water come up and splash over us. Once we were completely soaked, we retreated up to the shade of a tree to let the warm afternoon sun dry us off.

I was staring straight up at the sky between two palm trees, literally without a care, when I heard a familiar sound. It was Anna's cell phone and she answered it. The sound of her voice, the hum of other conversations on the beach, the rhythm of the waves lapping up on the beach, oh, how peaceful.

When I awoke, it was time to get dressed for a concert. We would be going to the Waikiki Shell to hear the Beach Boys preceded by some kind of tribute to Eddie. I had almost no idea who he was or why, as they say in Hawaii, "Eddie would go," or where he went or if he ever came back, but all of this we would find out that night.

We thought about walking from the New Otani to the Waikiki Shell for the Beach Boys Concert. After all, you could see it from our window. Taking into consideration that we were eight stories up and the park doesn't have that many trees, it appeared to be close by. But I wasn't taking any chances.

I dropped off Anna, drove back to the hotel, parked the SUV and walked back to where she was saving us a place in the line. The tickets said 6 p.m. and we were right on time, but the Beach Boys themselves would not be taking the stage until 8 p.m.

So what would we be seeing for two hours? It would be a program about Hokule'a, a cross between a boat and an outrigger canoe that was built as a testimony to the bravery and ingenuity of the ancient Polynesian sailors who set out to find other islands, like the Hawaiian Islands.

They came, we were told, from Tahiti and the program that July night in 2006 would raise funds for the program and commemorate one particular sail, one taken in 1978, that ended with the craft capsizing in turbulent waters in the Molokai Channel. With the prospects of rescue looking dim, Eddie Aikau, a local surfer and lifeguard, took his long board and paddled off for help.

That's the Eddie of "Eddie Would Go," a popular saying in the islands to this day. Unfortunately, he was lost at sea and his body was never found. The rest of the crew was saved the next day. The tribute, along with speeches, singing, hula dancing, an introduction of the members of the original crew, news footage shown on a giant screen and, finally, a moment of silence took up the entire two hours.

The Beach Boys bounded up to the stage of the Waikiki Shell late and you could just tell that they were miffed. It took them an hour to get themselves and the crowd into the mood and, then, at exactly 10 p.m., the lead singer Mike Love said tersely, "You've all heard about the noise ordinance," and the boys fled without another word or strum of the guitar.

It must have been very disappointing for one elderly lady in a big plastic hat who must have been the Beach Boys' biggest fan. She was sitting right in front of Anna, so we traded places because I could see just over her hat and get a good view of "boys in the band." But then she stood up and started swaying, well, jerking to and fro would be more accurate, to the sounds of the surf hits from the past and my vision was blocked.

Then it started raining and the old girl sought refuge under her umbrella, which shot up as the drops started to fall. So I had a good time peeking through the gap between the umbrella and the young girl who sat next to her. In spite of the weather, everyone seemed to be in good spirits. Then the clock struck 10:00 and the party ended.

Anna and I joined the rest of the crowd as we walked through Kapiolani Park, which basked in the glow of the lights from the "shell" behind us and the tennis courts ahead of us. We dodged a couple of bums then ran into a phalanx of four-wheel vehicles with their lights out, policemen atop them just waiting for trouble. We didn't give them any.

We agreed that the boat tribute went on way too long and, while the people around us were pretty good-natured, Anna did say, "If I heard that kid behind us say, 'Sucks' one more time, I was going to turn around and slap him. Look, no matter who was playing or what kind of music it was, there you were at Waikiki with a full moon over Diamond Head... most of the time anyway. What more could you ask for?"

Of course I agreed and we strolled under the full moon that had reappeared just for us and heard, off in the distance, the sound of the waves. We might have stopped under a palm tree but, thinking about that poor couple up at Round Top, we marched at a pretty good clip to get back to the New Otani.

The Ala Moana Shopping Center in Honolulu is huge. We found that out on Sunday, July 9, 2006. First of all, it is so enormous that we found it with no trouble at all. Secondly, we couldn't find our car when we wanted to leave.

I tried on my own with Anna waiting at the Honolulu Coffee Co. on the third floor. I knew it was in one of the lower levels and the number one came to mind so I walked around in that area pushing the horn button on the remote.

When Anna called to find out what was taking so long and heard my sad story, she insisted on joining in the search. About an hour later, by retracing our steps from the moment we first arrived at this monstrosity of a mall, we found the exact elevator that took us to the surface after we parked.

Lo and behold, there it was, waiting for us the whole time. And to think, we'd begun to suspect it had been stolen.

As we drove back to the New Otani, we saw a big screen on the beach and a crowd and food stands. Sunset on the beach. What a sight. As frazzled as we were, we still couldn't stay away. We walked along the stone wall that runs between the ocean and the Aquarium toward all the commotion. A film crew from the television series "Lost" was setting up a shot right in front of us.

We sat on a low wall facing Queen's Beach, eating a Philly sandwich and a Greek chicken wrap as a three piece band, two guitars and a trombone, let loose with some hard rock.

Then the movie began on the big screen. It was about the Yukon and snow and huskies. A perfect contrast to the palm trees swaying in the evening breeze. But we didn't come all this way to see a movie, so we made our way back toward the hotel and were finally able to laugh about our adventure at the Ala Moana.

The next day we went back to the famous Hanauma Bay, which had been full on our first attempt to visit. There was plenty of room that Monday and Anna sat on the beach and watched me flop out into the water with my water sandals on. I had on a baseball cap and a snorkel apparatus, which turned out to be entirely unnecessary because, just as the guide book says, the fish swirled at my feet.

Our plan was to stay longer, but then an announcement was heard. Get out! A storm is coming and the water is too rough. Wouldn't you know it. Well, we obeyed and spent the rest of the day packing for our departure the next day.

But we did have one last Hawaiian moment, a luau at the Royal Hawaiian, known affectionately as "The Pink Lady of the Pacific." It was everything we expected, an overwhelming dinner, a good show, the perfect sunset, a little dancing and some interesting conversation with our fellow tourists.

4

The Last Leg of the Journey

The Sunshine State was wrapped in clouds that February day as our plane started its descent into Miami. George Stanley was not interested in the view. Unperturbed by the captain's orders, the flight attendant's request and common sense, he stood in the aisle with the overhead bin open and rummaged through his luggage. Finally, he finished whatever he was doing and sat down, much to my relief. His wife Eileen tried very hard not to react to this latest burst of nervous energy.

Once freed from the aircraft and given a cursory, "Bye now. Have a nice day," I checked on the status of the connecting flight from Miami to Santiago, Dominican Republic. When I first received my itinerary, I estimated the layover in Miami as "all day," and didn't even bother to put an exact number of hours to it. The large screen with the departure times and destinations blinked, updated itself and reassured me.

"Plenty of time," I said to myself. An entire afternoon stretched before me. Plenty of time to get lost before finding the right gate. An airport the size of Miami's is more than big enough for me to wander around, ask directions from several people, check a map, march off in the completely opposite direction, correct myself and then finally, almost accidentally, find what I'm looking for.

But first, I wanted to buy a glass of orange juice and raise it toward the person who poured it for me and say, "Here's to John McPhee."

In the mid-1960's, John McPhee went down to Florida to research the subject of oranges and orange juice for a magazine article. When he was done, his manuscript was long enough to become a 150 page book, which I carried with me. Simply entitled, *Oranges*, the classic was filled with all kinds of details on the subject. Day-dreaming about my trip to a tropical paradise, I had marked some of these fascinating facts in the hopes that someone would hear my toast and ask, "Who?"

"The word orange evolved from Sanskrit," John McPhee told me in the pages of his book. Coincidentally, a town, Aurenja, in southern France sounded like the word orange and, in time, that's how the Netherlands came under the rule of "The House of Orange." It's all there in his book.

"The history of Florida is measured in freezes," McPhee wrote as he ticked them off, 1747, 1766, 1774 and, 1835, but the big one came in 1895. Only the groves in Keystone City survived and the grateful townsfolk promptly renamed the place Frostproof.

"Oranges and orange blossoms have long been symbols of love," McPhee discovered and provided ample proof. He also noted that Renaissance artists depicting the life of Christ used backgrounds, not of Palestine, but of the Italian countryside and always included oranges, which were never grown in the time or place where Jesus actually lived.

Medieval superstitions about oranges and women were confusing. One held that the worst thing that could happen to an orange was the touch of a woman. Just her presence and a healthy tree would shed its fruit, then its leaves and finally crumble to the ground. But the temptation was irresistible for a woman because eating an orange would "banish all evil thoughts from her mind."

Explorers from Europe took orange seeds with them to the "New World," and spread them around liberally. It is assumed that Ponce de Leon performed this service for Florida, but the 1835 freeze killed almost every tree that took root since 1513. The theory back then was that an iceberg had broken free and floated all the way down to the waters off St. Augustine and caused this disaster. Only the trees on Merrit Island between the Indian River and the Banana River were spared.

The grove on the Indian River attracted growers and characters from all over the world. One of them was Jenny Anheuser, the daughter of the St. Louis brewer (as in Anheuser-Busch), who, along with her husband, arrived in the area in 1881. But, for some reason, the two of them assumed the identity of Italian nobility and he told everyone to call him Duc di Castellucio. They built a villa for themselves and nearly all the rooms were octagons, eight sided, but then they quarreled and built a wall right down the middle of the mansion and never spoke to one another again.

The oranges from the Indian River area became so famous that the Federal Trade Commission had to emit an order in the 1930's to try and limit the use of that name. The region in question is defined by McPhee as a 15-mile swath starting ten miles north of Daytona Beach and extending down to around Palm Beach.

Oh there's more. Much more. And I was itching to tell someone about it. I took the plastic cup of orange juice placed before me and, with a bit of ceremony, raised it toward the young man behind the counter. "To John McPhee," I announced. As the sweet juice passed my lips, I heard him say, "That'll be two dollars. Who's next?"

Some cities are identified with a song. Tony Bennett left his heart in one. Frank Sinatra's "my kind of town," is different from the one where, if you can make it there, you can make it anywhere. And I'm sure there are plenty set in or dedicated to Miami, Florida, but the one that circulates in my brain is Jimmy Buffett's, "Everybody's Got A Cousin in Miami."

In the album, "Fruitcakes," released in 1994 or thereabouts, I learned that Miami, "started out as a trading post, home to the Seminole pirate and pioneer... between the river of grass and the old Mosquito Coast before the railroad claimed the southernmost frontier."

What I knew about the place could be summed up in those few words, but I was about to learn a lot more from author Mark Derr. Raised in Florida, he had returned to the state in 1987 to write a book entitled, "Some Kind of Paradise, A Chronicle of Man and the Land in Florida."

First of all, the place was originally named Fort Dallas. What a coincidence! I just flew in from Dallas. The Calusa, a tribe of natives in the region, called Biscayne Bay, "Mayaimi," which meant "Big Water," and that just had a better sound to it so businessmen trying to promote the region adopted the name Miami.

Only a few people came this way with the idea of simply enjoying the scenery, much less preserving it. The history of Florida is a revelation of what unbridled greed can do. Whole tribes of peaceful exotic peoples were wiped out to make way for hotels. The land itself came under attack by plants brought from other places. Idiotic theories like draining the Everglades were set into motion without a single thought about the damage that would be done. And the impression I'd held that the state had been dragged into the Confederacy by the force of geography proved to be completely untrue.

I've been told that insanity is the distance between image and reality. So, if you want to preserve your Disneyworld image of Florida, then avoid books like Mark Derr's. He puts the state under an unforgiving microscope of fact and peering into it will flabbergast you.

At one point, I looked up to find a group of youngsters sitting across from me. Backpacks were stacked underfoot and cell phones were grasped in their palms. I had an almost uncontrollable urge to cry out, "Hey! Have you ever heard of Chief Coacoochee who said, 'The white man may chain our hands and feet, but the red man's heart will always be free'? He was the son of Chief Miccosukee." If I had given voice to my thoughts, I'm almost sure one of them would have replied, "Oh yeah, the casino. I've heard of it."

Looking out the windows of the terminal, I thought about Emilio and Emma and the vacations we spent visiting them in Coral Gables.

My father-in-law, Lupercio Arroyo, first married when he was a young man and that union produced a girl, Emma. Lupercio divorced and remained single for decades until he met my mother-in-law, Isabel, and they were married in 1950. So the age difference between my wife Anna and her half sister Emma was about 30 years. Nonetheless, they got along pretty well, and their relationship matured as the years went by. In fact, when our first child, Anisa, was born in 1979, Emma and her husband Emilio Salguero came out to California and visited us.

We took them up to San Francisco and Anisa cried all the way and most of the return trip as well. And she wasn't the only one who misbehaved. I recall being at a cafeteria style diner and Emma swept an ash tray off the table and into her large purse. When she saw the expression on my face, she said, "A souvenir. They expect you to take it."

"Would you like the silverware too?" I chuckled. "How about one of the chairs? I'm sure they'd want you to have that too." I wasn't being sarcastic. At least I didn't think I was. I was just being funny. At least I thought I was. Emma and Anna glared at me. Emilio howled in laughter and got a death stare himself. The two of us got along just fine after that.

A native of Cuba, Emilio worked as a longshoreman on the docks in New York and always assumed he could return to his island some day. But Fidel Castro came along and the closest the Salguero's ever got to Cuba was Coral Gables in Florida. Emilio stood at least half a foot taller than me, had an enormous barrel chest that he loved to uncover, displaying this thick mat of black hair, and all that weight was carried along on two thin, smooth legs that extended out of a pair of shorts he seemed to wear everywhere.

Emma was tiny in comparison. So thin that her eyes seemed extraordinarily large and she spoke in a husky voice, probably the result of years of smoking. Whenever she called out to California to talk to Anna and got the answering machine, that voice would leave this message, "Emma."

When she'd call back, Anna would catch up with her sister, but then there would be complete silence punctuated by a "Uh oh!" or a "Oh no!" or "I knew it!' My wife would smile and tell us, "She's watching a novela on TV."

When Anisa was about ten years old and her sister, Amanda, must have been seven, we flew back to Florida to visit Emma and Emilio in Coral Gables. They took us to the beach one day and dropped the four of us off so we could enjoy the surf and sun while they went off to buy something for dinner later on. So this family of four trudged through the sand and set up camp in the midst of friendly groups of fellow bathers.

Anna isn't much for the water so she kept watch as the two girls and I frolicked in the water. Then a couple of women, topless, walked by holding hands. And the group of men next to Anna began posing for one another. "Hey, that looks great on you. Have you been working out?" And slowly it dawned on my wife. "Jim!" she screamed. "Jim! Come here! Now! We've got to go! Come on girls!"

But we were having such a good time. And so were the two topless women who'd decided to splash each other just a few yards from us. But we obeyed and soon were back at the spot where Emma and Emilio said they'd pick us up. "Oh yes," a lady confirmed, "that is the gay beach. Everyone knows. See that hotel right there? Well, that's where they stay and the beach is right here. Very nice tourists. Good tips."

When Anna explained to Emma, including the "everyone knows," her sister shrugged and said, "I didn't know. How would I know? We don't go to the beach." I struggled to keep a straight face, but Emilio just roared.

Our evenings in their Coral Gables home revolved around a Spanish-language soap opera, "Maria La Del Barrio," which could be translated as, "Mary, She of the Neighborhood." Actually, we had been watching this classic back home in California and were acquainted with the story line. The difference between Emma and us was that we didn't take it seriously.

So when we watched the wicked Zoraya trying to escape Mexico in a jet, Emma trembled with rage. After all, Zoraya had stabbed Maria's son, pushed some child in a wheelchair down a flight of stairs, beat up a witness to the event and that was just in the past week. And now, the evil Zoraya was getting away!

From over in the corner of the room, Emma heard me say, "Don't worry. That airplane is turning around. See how they're indicating that with the light coming in through the windows?" Emma shot Anna a look that said, "Shut that man up!" Anna relayed that message quite effectively.

One day, Anisa, teary-eyed, asked Anna, "Why are they fighting?" And Anna cocked an ear in the direction of all that shouting and said, "Oh no honey, that's not fighting. They're just talking. They always talk that way. Maybe they don't hear very well."

On another trip to visit Emma and Emilio, we stayed at a hotel in the center of Miami Beach and then, every day, drove over to Coral Gables.

Early one morning, our younger child Amanda, who was maybe all of ten years old at the time, and I strode out of the the hotel and walked down the street to Wolfie's, a world famous eatery on Miami Beach.

Unfortunately, the place was an hour away on foot. If we had simply turned around and walked in the other direction, we would have found a place called, "Einstein's" just a block away. But we didn't. Instead, we "pressed on," as I kept repeating to Amanda, almost all the way to South

Beach. Finally, this usually very cooperative and patient little girl plopped down on a bench and announced, "I'm not taking another step!"

We found a telephone booth (oh, those ancient times before cell phones) and she called the hotel, begging her mother to come and rescue her from this torture. And Anna did. The van arrived with Anisa laughing at our discomfort and the four of us drove about as many blocks as Amanda and I had walked to find this fabled Wolfie's place.

A few days after the Wolfie's disaster, I set off alone for breakfast and ended up walking into a very impressive building which had a cafeteria on the ground floor. In fact, you could see the people at their tables through large windows as you walked by on the sidewalk. That's what drew me inside. It was a buffet and you simply picked up a plate and set off down aisles and aisles of eggs, sausages, pancakes and toast.

The waiter came by and filled a coffee cup, gave me a little nod and a shrug. I smiled at him and expressed my thanks. He continued on his way. When I had my fill of this feast, I caught his eye once again and he approached.

"I've never been here before," I said. "Where do you pay?"

"You don't sir. This is a residence hotel. Are you a resident? Or a visitor? Which resident are you visiting?"

I had just eaten at a senior citizen retirement hotel. And no one had stopped me. The waiter let me escape perhaps thinking I was a deranged but harmless tourist. I hurried back to our hotel, ran into the room where my wife and children were asleep and examined my face in the bathroom mirror. It was a couple of days before I told them about my experience and I never went off alone again.

Emma and Emilio were no longer with us and the house in Coral Gables fell victim to the 2008 real estate financing crisis so, instead of going out to see them, I bought a Cuban sandwich and thought of those days.

The unending CNN newscast continued on the television sets popping out of the ceiling, but no one was watching it because the time to board was fast approaching. The call was indistinct and the trumpet muffled  (to use a Biblical reference), so the passengers simply mobbed the two women checking boarding passes and pushed their way through to the tunnel leading to the plane.

I had no choice but to go in almost last and, as I stepped into the aircraft, heard the tumult of many voices speaking three languages but all saying the same thing. "Which seat is mine? That one? No? That one? All the way back there?" But I'm just guessing on one of those tongues based on facial expressions and frantic gestures.

The warnings and explanations about flotation devices and emergency exits went virtually unheard. It seemed the crew had lost all control, but didn't seem upset about it. After all, they do this job every single day and they knew something I didn't. When the plane actually started to move, the passengers who had been standing in the aisles, crouching on seats, bouncing their children on their knees, shouting at one another suddenly shut up and plopped down for take-off.

I occupied a window seat and the older couple sitting next to me had their heads bowed. When the airplane lifted off the ground, the woman shouted, "God lives!" and clapped. Others joined in and then, long before the captain finished welcoming them to relax and enjoy the flight to Santiago, the passengers renewed their standing, crouching, bouncing and shouting.

We Watrous' are not a traveling tribe. From the very beginning, I could see that my parents were more comfortable with a routine and, even with the promise of good times, they found it hard to pick up and go someplace merely for the fun of it.

I do recall the summer we went north from the Connecticut coastline through Massachusetts and up into Maine with the Moon family. That was their name. Delightful, isn't it? John and Orchis (although we pronounced it Auchis), were the parents of a family with exactly the same number of children as ours. My mother and Orchis would match each other until eventually both families had about a half dozen kids each.

We all stayed in an enormous house on a lake. The porch encircled the old place and it was completely screened in to protect us from the mosquitoes. My older brother and I, along with the Moon boy, Scott, would venture down these paths that led to a lake, while the younger boys found things to do closer to home. Poor Carolyn had to help her mother take care of the younger boys. Our fathers, in the meantime, had sallied forth before dawn, headed down to the water to fish.

There are only two scenes of that trip that survive in my memory. In the first, we boys break out of the woods, climb a dune of sawdust and race to the shoreline where our fathers are expertly putting lures on their lines. The second is of my mother, pregnant with another child, my sister I believe, climbing over some rocks on the Maine shore to pick up a starfish.

Our departure from Connecticut to California in 1959, followed in 1960 by our quick return to New England, only to end with our final westward trek back to the Golden State does not count as vacation travel. It was not even a picnic, believe me.

We were about an hour away from Santiago when the flight crew distributed two papers to each adult passenger. This was solid proof that I had, for the first time really, traveled beyond the boundaries of the United States.

A day in Ensenada, Mexico during a three-day cruise from Long Beach didn't count and neither did a night looking for a lobster dinner in a border town south of San Diego.

Studying the four inch by six inch questionnaires, I was tempted to say out loud, "Declare something? Why yes. I do declare I'm hungry." But everyone else was taking this very seriously which, up to that point, hadn't been the case.

All those rules about the size of carry-ons, where they could be stowed, the seat belts, the overhead bins, the electronic devices, children kicking the backs of seats (some of these regulations were unwritten but nonetheless important) had been completely ignored. The only thing that brought some order to the entire flight experience was the mere fact that it got dark outside and one after another, they all succumbed to sleep.

The Dominican Republic wanted to know a bit about me and my motives for entering the country, how much money I brought with me and if fresh fruit and vegetables were stuffed in my luggage. I had ready answers to all of those questions. The second sheet asked for more specifics, my passport number, where I planned on staying, for how long and if I wanted cream and sugar in my coffee.

In my typical "good student" fashion, I raised my hand with the papers clutched therein, waiting for the flight attendant to congratulate me on being the first in my class to finish the exam. He merely pursed his lips, shook his head and said, "At customs…when we land." There were other hands, other papers, other Americans like me who had to be told and he moved down the aisle to do so.

From that point on, chaos returned as people began gathering up their possessions in anticipation of the landing. They craned their necks to see the lights of the city coming into view and jostled their peacefully dozing children, who screamed in protest. Once fully awake, the youngsters wandered off like little puppies, curiously sniffing around and smiling at strangers.

But they all knew what was happening and I didn't. See, I expected a few announcements from the captain. A couple of, "Well, ladies and gentlemen, we are now within a half hour of our destination. Please remain seated as we…" And then, about 15 minutes later, "And you can see the city of Santiago off to your left. It's overcast, temperature around 70 and the time is…"

But our captain remained silent and apparently I was the only one who even expected him to advise us of the plane's progress. Suddenly, as far as I was concerned, the landing gear clunked into place and we were descending toward a runway marked by rows of lights. The actual touchdown was greeted by applause and shouts of joy, as well as praise to God and Jesus.

And then a woman's voice sang out. "Ladies and gentlemen," she said in Spanish. "We have landed in Santiago de los Caballeros, Republica Dominicana. Please remain seated until the captain…" The rest was drowned out by the rumble of voices, the unlatching of overhead bins, the shouts to children and from children, the zipping and unzipping of carryon bags.

Wisely, the flight crew retreated to the back of the plane and the very front as the passengers departed. I followed their lead and waited for just about everyone else to abandon ship before shuffling forward. The captain and crew lounged at the cockpit door, having run out of enthusiastic goodbye's for the night and simply waved as I went by with what I thought was a polite nod and slight bow.

Emerging from the tunnel leading into the terminal, I was ushered toward the Customs and Immigration line, where one of the papers I'd filled out on board was collected, along with $10 for a tourist card. Not ten steps later, I was asked for that card. Believe me, I was tempted to laugh and make some remark, but it was late. No one seemed to be in the mood for a witty observation, least of all the man ahead of me who didn't have $10 in cash.

He had tried to explain why he had flown into the country without having the courtesy of carrying cash for the tourist card. I gathered that he was being told to leave his computer and other possessions there at the counter, go outside the terminal to an automatic teller machine, try to coax the some folding money out of it, go through security to re-enter the building, although at this late hour, the detail of uniformed guards had already left for the night, come back to this very counter and turn over the money and then we'll give you your computer and whatever else you brought with you.

The man behind him in line, which was me, understood completely what was expected of him. I pulled another $10 bill out of my wallet and handed it to him. "Here you go," I said in English, which seemed to be his primary language.

He couldn't thank me enough. The people behind the counter had seen this all before and they waited for the dialogue between us to end, took both $10 bills and waved us into the next stage of confusion, the baggage claim area.

This was, at least, familiar to me. Luggage of all sizes and colors tumbled out of the chute in the middle of a chrome carousel as passengers jockeyed for position. Carts, which usually cost you something at airports in the

United States, are available for free and that's the reason I took one. I only had one bag, but I didn't want to be the only guy without a cart.

We had arrived hours behind schedule but, in the excitement of retrieving my bag, I didn't have the presence of mind to check a clock. The watch on my hand was now useless. Just before landing, I realized it had not only stopped but that the winding stem had fallen out at some point. Well, at an exact point, 9:43 p.m.

The only sound being made at the Cibao International Airport came from those of us who had just arrived because the carousel ground to a stop when the last bag slid into view. It was mine. Up to that point, I hadn't noticed the police dogs. But one of them came up to me and sniffed, then gave the clothing packed in my luggage another sniff. Unimpressed, he trotted away. The uniformed man at the end of a leash followed him.

For a second, I wondered what happened when Anna arrived, because it is her practice to carry dog treats in her carryon bag as a way to greet the Chihuahuas who live with our hosts.

Surely, the German shepherds are well-trained and seek only contraband, not bite-sized morsels. But wouldn't it have been funny...

Speaking of Mrs. Watrous, I wondered where she might be at that moment. Outside on the curb, anxiously waiting for her man to push through the glass doors, she would be peering around others who'd come to greet their loved ones.

"There he is! There he is!" she would shout. "Oh, how long has it been? Just a week? It seemed like an eternity!"

But she would have to wait because I still had the second paper and it would be taken by a man standing in front of an x-ray machine. Taking both of my bags, he plopped them on the conveyer belt, then held out a hand for the document, which he immediately put in a basket filled with similar papers and pointed to a line of people.

Once my possessions and my person had been probed with these invasive rays of light, we were both cleared to exit the airport terminal and enter the paradise that waited just steps away.

But no, not yet. A young man had grabbed both my bags, caught my eye and said, in his best English, "Follow me." Now what? Was I to be interrogated? Had I caused some offense by packing underwear that might disintegrate in the tropical heat? And the hat. It must be the hat. I had packed a crushable, all purpose floppy hat to keep the warm sun from blistering my bald pate. Was that considered bad form?

Having my bags captive, the young man also had me in tow and he led me to a door, which he shoved open and suddenly, I was outside, on the curb, where friends and family scanned the arriving passengers. I took a closer look and realized this wasn't an authority figure, but a courtesy attendant, a nice young man who toted tourists' bags in hopes of a tip. I would not disappoint him and pulled out three one-dollar bills.

"Is U.S. currency acceptable?" I asked in Spanish. His immediate acceptance of the gratuity indicated it was. And his grin and appreciative nod told me I had probably set the record for that week or at least that flight. He stayed at my side as I bobbed my head from side to side, looking into the mass of faces, expecting to see a familiar face.

"Are you Jim?" asked a man I'd never seen before in my life. He waved a magazine, *La Atalaya*, in one hand and an envelope in the other. "Anna sent me to get you."

5

Welcome to Santiago

My name is Danny," said the man. I estimated his age at 40, but it is hard to judge, in my opinion, when someone has skin as dark as his. With the pale complexion I have, anyone can see the wrinkles, the splotches, the gray whiskers  that sprout out everywhere and figure that I am over 60 years of age. But not so with Danny, whose chocolate-colored hue hid his exact age quite well.

"I'm a brother," were the next words he spoke. I was glad to hear of our tight relationship because now he had my bags in his hands. "This way."

As we got beyond the lights of the airport terminal, I must admit to a moment of apprehension, but he had the same magazine I get. The same one we study as a congregation every Sunday. The same one we have distributed from door to door for over a hundred years and I have personally since the age of ten. Actually, *The Watchtower* gets into about 40 million hands a month all over the world. So this is absolute proof Danny is associated with me and I can trust him.

Wait a minute!

The envelope!

A message from Anna. "Your plane was delayed and we had to get to the resort by a specific check-in time so Danny will take you in his taxi to the house and let you in. He has the key, which you keep, and then, in the morning, around 9 a.m., he will come back to get you and take you to the bus station. Here's the ticket to Puerto Plata. When you get there, take the shuttle to the resort, because that's the only way you can get in right now. I'll explain why when you get here. Taxi's aren't allowed to drop off for some reason."

"Take the battery out of your cell phone after you turn it off because any incoming calls cost a fortune here."

And then came some specific instructions on where I was to sleep, what cupboards I could open and a warning that there isn't much hot water available for showering and that I shouldn't drink any water except from the pitcher in the refrigerator.

Danny, my brother, flipped open the trunk and laid my luggage in carefully, then opened the driver's door with his key. He pointed to the other side of the car and I obeyed his directions.

"Everything all right? No problems?" Danny inquired with a lilting, halting rhythm. "Don't worry. We'll be there right away. It's only about 30 minutes this time of night."

I noticed that seat belts were available but obviously not mandatory. There was nothing in or on the vehicle to indicate it was a taxi and Danny seemed to notice that I noticed.

"Taxi drivers are trying to form a union," he explained. "They don't like guys like me because we don't have the same permit." I took that to mean Danny had no permit of any kind. He'd just decided one day that his car was available for hire.

"I didn't want to drive a taxi," he continued. "I had a job but the factory closed and, when I couldn't find work, my cousin told me, 'Be a taxi.' You just buy the sign," and he jerked his head toward the back seat, where I could see two or three articles that would lead one to believe this car was a taxi, "and just start driving."

"There are conchos," he continued, "but they all have their routes and I didn't like the idea of picking up people on the street, squashing them into my car for a few pesos. This is better."

Putting it all together in my own mind, I said, "So actually, you're like a limousine. People call you and you go pick them up from the airport or wherever. I get it."

Danny squinted at me. "Sure. Just like that."

We were making good time because Danny didn't stop for signs or lights. He slowed down, of course, but never came to a complete stop. Again, he sensed my concern.

"This time of night, we don't dare stop. That's when you might get robbed."

Oh, that's comforting.

"We're almost there. See, there's the monument."

Yes, I saw it. Hard to miss. Situated on a hill, lit up in colors that rotated between pink, blue, white and green, the tower was an impressive sight.

Danny made an unexpected left turn, a quick right, another left and then came to an abrupt stop. "We're here."

We were on a residential street with every house protected by a fortress-like array of iron spires. In the dark, I couldn't appreciate the bright colors, the friendly atmosphere, the exotic setting that I would discover over the next couple of weeks. At that point, it looked like I was being booked into jail.

Danny led the way up a flight of tile stairs to a first landing, where he inserted one of the keys into a padlock and then swung an iron gate back so I could pass. Then he carefully closed the gate and scooted around me so he could open the next gate that guarded the front door. Using the same key, he gained entry and, with a sweep of his hand, still holding my carry-on, bade me to enter.

Switching roles from taxi driver to concierge, my new friend took me from living room to dining room to kitchen and repeated just about everything Anna had written in her letter, emphasizing the "don't drink the water out of the tap," and then reassured me he'd be back in a few hours.

When I pulled out another $3 in U.S. currency, Danny did something that never again happened in the Dominican Republic the entire time I was there. He said, "Oh no, Brother Jim, that's not necessary. Sister Anna took care of that already. Get some rest. And there's food in the refrigerator if you're hungry. Remember, only that water."

I should have been exhausted, but my internal clock had me four or five hours off schedule. So instead of the 1:30 I saw on the clock, it was really 9:30 or 8:30 the day before or would that be 5:30 today? Taking no chances on the water, I removed from the refrigerator a green bottle with a label that read, "Presidente," on it. In finer print, "Cerveza," and what a fine brew it was.

It would do no good to describe the rooms at this point because, in the light of day, and with other people there, they never looked exactly as they did that night. In my memory, I recall a kitchen with a café style table, three chairs around it, with a view of a living room with a futon arranged like a sofa and two wicker chairs. Sitting at that kitchen table, I could see a hallway to the left leading to, I imagined, a bedroom or two

The president and I kissed a few times and then I had to excuse myself to go to the bathroom, which was, of course, on the right, just as John Fogarty said when he tried to say, "Bad moon on the rise."

The futon looked fine to me just the way it was so I never tried to flatten it out, just took my ease there until I awoke to unusual sounds.

A humming chatter slowly reaching the level of a roar came floating in through the shutters. When I opened one of them, expecting to see glass, I realized there wasn't any. All the windows were like that. The great part was that not a single insect took advantage of this opportunity. All that entered was sunlight, fresh air and, of course, the noise.

Have you ever lived close to an elementary school and at recess heard the sound of many children laughing and shouting? That was one element of what I heard. But there was also automobile horns squawking and whooping not that far away. And then a motorcycle whirred around a nearby corner and a deep, almost guttural, voice sang out. "Listin Diario." Even though I'd never heard that expression before, there was no mistaking the words. What diction. What articulation. And while riding on a motorcycle.

A woman, a contralto, joined the opera and cried out, in Spanish, "I have avocados. I have papayas. I have bananas. I have squashes. I have beans. Guandules!"

But all that, as lovely as it was, was drowned out by a truck-sounding vehicle with a bullhorn mounted somewhere, through which a voice announced that batteries were for sale. All kinds of batteries. There must be, I decided, a great need for batteries.

El Presidente had nothing left to offer, so I removed him from office and made coffee, using the water from the refrigerator as instructed. It was as I rummaged around looking for a cup that I glanced at the clock. Only 6 a.m.? So for me, it would be 11 a.m. or maybe 2 a.m. I was sure the caffeine would help clear things up on that count.

No matter really because Danny would be here in about three hours, long enough for me to find out that one can take a shower in water that starts out cold, then lukewarm, then very cold. Later, I would find out that there is a a tiny device attached to the nozzle that will warm the water just long enough to have a pleasant bathing experience.

Re-examining the living room a bit, I came to suspect this was not where Anna and I would be staying. A quick search of the back bedrooms, both of them, turned up no luggage associated with Mrs. Watrous. Then, it dawned on me that there was another door in the kitchen.

I opened it and found a washer and dryer in a room with iron bars (of course) and another door. I knocked. No answer. I timidly pushed it open to find the exact same kitchen only turned in the opposite direction, followed by the living room and, instead of a hallway, three doors. The middle one turned out to be the bathroom. The other two were bedrooms. The one on the right was where I found evidence of my wife's presence.

And, although I was absolutely sure everything was fine, that Danny was my "brother," and this was where I should be and I was secure behind these bars, the corroboration was comforting.

The refrigerator on "our" side had a pitcher of water as well and a few more green bottles with the presidential seal, as well as some bread, butter and jam. The beer would come in handy upon our return from the resort but, right now, I whipped up a simple sandwich.

Toast would have been even better, but as I've said before, every job begins with a search and I didn't find the toaster soon enough so I was content with what I had.

Back in the "other" kitchen, I replenished my coffee cup and came upon, in the corner, an old friend. The television!

Morning programs in the Dominican Republic turned out to be a series of talk shows where a host talks and talks and talks. No guests. No interviews. No cutting away to on-the-spot reporters. None of that. Just a man, sitting at a small desk, rattling off one complaint after another. There's a telephone on the desk but it never rang and he never made a call either.

Farther along the dial, some more familiar programs appeared, some of them in English, others dubbed into Spanish and I probably would have been entertained for the hour or so until Danny showed up, but I had become aware of the fact that I was not alone.

A door slowly opened and a head peeked around to see who was making all that noise. It was a small dog, a Chihuahua, and, in due course, a second one joined him. They bristled at my presence, but then shrugged off their irritation and tip-toed to the front door. I opened it and they headed off to take care of their necessities. In due course, they returned, ignored me and went back to wherever they'd spent the night.

Outside on the terrace, I took my first look at my surroundings and realized that there were three apartments, one at street level and the other two at the top of the stairs.

On a third level was a set of goal posts with three wires strung up between them, obviously the place where clothes were hung out to dry and a large metal tank, which I later learned is called a "tinaco" and holds an emergency supply of water should the city system fail.

From that vantage point, I could see similar apartment houses up and down the street, but the one directly across from me had a large orange tile roof fitted over all of its features. The rest of us would fry out in the afternoon sun but this one neighbor had this charming and useful addition.

Then I heard Danny hail me from the street and the two of us were soon on our way north, out of Santiago to the all-inclusive resort in Puerto Plata.

In the short drive from the neighborhood called El Ensueno to the bus station, I was amazed at the number of people on the street, the tiny motorcycles weaving through traffic and the "conchos" darting to the curb to pick up passengers and then, oblivious to any danger, barging right back out to the middle of the street.

The motorcycles carried, beside the driver, at least one other person, maybe two and sometimes they balanced long pipes, propane tanks, a pane of glass or planks of wood on their shoulders.

"Brother Jim," the driver laughed. "Don't worry. I'll get you there."

Of that I had no doubt, I replied, but what, how, why... all of this... what I'm seeing here... this anarchy?

"This is nothing. An hour from now, that's when it will really get interesting."

I asked about the lack of bicycles. Surely that would be an economic and more environmentally conscious mode of transportation.

"No. A Dominican would never pedal a bike. Too low for him. Besides, it's hot."

No arguing with that logic. And why so many people on each bike? I'd just seen a family of four whiz by. "Most are moto-taxi. See that one? Driver, man, woman and look... baby."

In that short distance, I saw a girl, no older than ten with her hair up in curlers, which were empty soda cans. And I learned that, for some people, there is no shame in littering, just throwing items out of an open car window or letting papers fall from your hands to the street. Neither is there anything to apologize for if one should stop in the street, press a finger against one nostril and snort out a stream of snot from the other.

Distracted by this insanity, I had to be told that we had arrived at the bus station, which surprised me by being quite modern and orderly. Danny correctly interpreted my reaction.

"You go on the good bus," he said. "There's another bus, which costs less and doesn't have air conditioning and the seats aren't as good either. So you got the luxury today."

And he was right. By any standard, the bus I boarded was first class. The seats were wider and more comfortable than the ones on the airplanes I'd been on for the last day and a half. Although my experience on trains is very limited, I still felt sure only a few compared favorably with the interior of this Dominican bus.

The driver went up and down the aisle, noting the rare empty seat and said we would be getting underway in just a few moments. It turned out that, when those few spots were filled, it was time to go. Actually, a most efficient system.

From my window seat, I could see, but not comprehend, the beauty and ugliness of Cibao, this northern region of the island. People crouched down at the banks of a stream that, even from a distance, could easily be described as polluted. In spite of the rocks, they walked in bare feet to shacks that perched on green hills. But, at the same time, if I scanned farther up the road, the view was one of a paradise.

As the bus made the wide turn around some mountain, tiny huts within mere feet of the asphalt pavement popped into view. The folks inside were selling coffee, beer, juice or whatever else might earn a few pesos and customers were actually lined up. Any wide spot turned out to be the perfect place for a swarm of those moto-taxis and the drivers, all young men, scanned for potential customers like bees in a constant search for pollen.

So engrossed I was in the sights that the sound of a man talking to me went unnoticed. "Your ticket!" he finally demanded in English. I jumped a bit and then reached into my jacket pocket and pulled it out. He nodded, accepted it, read it and handed it back to me, then continued on his way.

Everyone around me had me pegged for a lone tourist and they felt the polite thing to do was to leave me to my thoughts, which were many and jumbled as the bus continued north until it reached a station much like the one we left in Santiago.

As promised in the note Danny gave me, the shuttle identifying the resort (along with several others) was waiting within a yard or so from where we stepped down from the bus. These were tighter quarters but nonetheless quite adequate for the quick run toward the beaches and hotels that have been built for visitors like me.

The driver made announcements and advisements in a language I believed was English but the sound system garbled his speech to the point where I had no idea what he was saying. Still, the fact we were making a hard right and going through a gate, which opened to let us in and then closed right behind us, led me to understand what he meant.

I thought of Danny when I saw the unmarked cars loitering at the entrance and realized why he hadn't just driven me these few hours up to the resort itself. A van with the side panels emblazoned with official-looking seals roared past us toward the gate and I could only imagine that the men inside were assigned to disperse the taxis.

The shuttle went from one resort to the next, each with an exotic-sounding name like "Blue Bay," "Lifestyles," "Shoreline Paradise," and then finally the one where I'd finally be joining my wife Anna.

6

Ah Luxury!

G reeted at the foot of the mini-bus by a man in a pith helmet, I was impressed by the enormous entrance to the place but couldn't help compare it to what I'd seen on the way. My hands were freed from my two bags so that I could be led to the marble counter where two quite attractive women gave me a warm good morning.

Within minutes, my wrist was adorned by a band, which I was never to remove… ever. Well, not until they cut it off when I was to be released back into the wild. All was going so well and then a young man came out of an office and asked for my "confirmation letter."

Having no idea what this letter would confirm nor in possession of such a paper, I stammered in Spanish, "Surely my wife has it. She's already here. Checked in yesterday some time. Wonderful woman. I'm sure you've met her."

The three of them conferred, tapped on the keys of a computer, huddled again, shook their heads, then turned back to me with I could only assume would be very bad news.

The man felt it was his duty to inform me that there was no such person of that name at the resort. Why I always look for the joke in everything is a mystery even to me, but I responded, "So the all-inclusive resort does not include my wife?"

The three of them tried to smile at my attempt at humor but then all of us heard, at the same time, a whistle, a sharp blast, and then one word... "Jim!"

"That," I smiled, "would be Mrs. Watrous."

The tension building at the counter vanished when we all discovered that the room we would occupy had been listed under the name of our friends. Understanding nods and hearty handshakes all around and then I hugged Anna because we hadn't seen each other in a while, of course, but also to prove to the staff that we were man and wife. Actually her greeting and the look on her face had already convinced them of that.

Not long thereafter, Anna and I sat down at a table in the main dining area. My plate overflowed with the fruits of a buffet breakfast and my wife of 40 years listened to my account of the trip. I started with the comedic flight attendant but left out all the commentary that went with the ensuing stops in Dallas and Miami.

"Everyone is down at the beach," said Anna, and soon we were too.

Tourists lounged behind sheer curtains hanging from elaborate structures, some raised up on platforms the size of a king-size bed and, from time to time, traipsed down to the cove, where they allowed the warm water to splash upon their bodies. And this would be the way most of our day would be spent.

Priti and Missy were familiar to me and I'd met Jerry and Linda before but couldn't remember exactly where.

"Idaho," said the man about 25 years younger than me. "That's where we met. Idaho Falls. But we moved to the Boise area since then."

Even in my imagination, I was reluctant to return to Idaho.

The first time we went there, my wife and two girls drove through the state to its eastern corner to visit the Idaho Falls, Blackfoot area. We even ventured into Wyoming to see Yellowstone National Park. A wonderful time.

I remember the day we stopped at the World Potato Expo. Not the Idaho Potato Center, nor the North American Potato Museum, but the W-O-R-L-D Potato Expo. We had seen the signs for miles, telling us not to miss this sight and, what's more, they offered, "Free Taters for Out of Staters," and I'd invariably hoot, "That's us!"

The years have passed and Blackfoot, Idaho must have changed since then, but I recalled that we drove past Elmer's Antiques and then Kountry Klub (a golf store) and finally an enormous metal statue of a young woman, dressed in a mini-skirt, wearing a feather in her hair and her right arm bent at the elbow. You could imagine her promising to tell the truth, the whole truth and nothing but the truth. I believe she has since disappeared from the cityscape or has been modified in some way.

But just beyond her, we found the railroad boxcar that was the home of the W.P.E. (World Potato Expo). The three words in gigantic letters, along with a massive model of a baked potato with sour cream and butter pouring out of it like lava from a volcano made it impossible to miss. We "out of staters" walked in and, within the first few seconds, were told that the suggested "donation" was $1.00.

We'd come so far that a $1 bill from each of the four of us plus our hosts, two ladies from the Idaho Falls area, didn't seem too much of an expense. What we got for our donation was a self-guided tour, in which we learned that the ancient Incas in South America are credited with planting the first potatoes. Then, there was the world's largest potato chip, kept under a clear plastic dome and the letters written by then-Vice President Dan Quayle and representatives of the Potato Lobby over the unfortunate misspelling of the plural form of potato by Quayle. It should be potatoes, not potatos.

We self-guided ourselves into what looked like a regular living room with couches, chairs and a television set, which broadcast for us the video, "The Glory of the Spud," a ten-minute documentary. When it was over, we all felt we had earned our "free tater" and the lady who took our dollars at the start of the tour realized we couldn't be stalled any longer. She'd seen the look on our faces before on other "out of staters" and led us quickly to the railroad car that had been tacked onto the back of the structure.

Three picnic tables and benches were arranged in the center of the room and the walls were filled with potato memorabilia, including the controversial "chocolate potato." The board that governs the W.P.E. has always maintained that everything offered at the site should be made from potatoes and, technically, this item did not meet that criteria. I could have investigated further, but we were summoned up to the counter to talk "free taters."

A young man with a sunburned face and a woman who could have been his mother greeted us heartily and said they were ready to prepare, for our dining pleasure, the spuds we had been promised by roadside signs ever since we entered the sovereign state of Idaho.

"Would you like anything other than butter and sour cream on your baked potato?" the young man asked.

"Oh, what do you have?"

Well, they've got everything, from cheese to broccoli to chili, you name it. "Each topping costs $1," he smiled.

I was very happy with my baked potato with sour cream and butter.

Of course I complain, but, overall, I loved the W.P.E. and would go back again. Happily, I would explore more carefully that chocolate potato brouhaha and maybe finally learn the difference between a "tuber" and a "legume."

The state of Idaho also provided me and my younger daughter, Amanda, with a cherished memory, which I share with you now.

She was 13 years old at the time and, while Anna and older sister Anisa stayed back at the house of our hosts, the two of us set off to find McDermott Field, home of the Idaho Falls Braves of the Class A Pioneer League, a first rung in the ladder leading up the Major Leagues. It took us 45 minutes to get there, not because of the size of the town, but because, as I kept telling Amanda, "The streets are laid out all wrong." Amanda kept turning the map in every direction, trying to get an accurate reading of where I'd taken her and we ended up at a spot within walking distance of our point of origin.

We hadn't missed too much. The barbershop quartet had crooned the national anthem and the Billings, Montana Mustangs were still batting in the top of the first. The smell of beer and cigars, freshly-cut grass, the mountains looming over the scoreboard, the chatter in the stands and the free ticket a teenager leaving the park gave me just as we arrived made me a happy tourist.

"Why are we sitting up here?" the youngster behind us asked the boy sitting next to him. "Why can't we be over there?"

"Because it's reserved, stupid. See the sign. It says, 'A A.' It's for the Alcoholics Anonymous. They must be on a field trip or something."

I turned to Amanda, who looked back at me wide-eyed and struggling to keep from giggling.

"So what do you think?" I asked her. "They've got a man on first, nobody out. Bunt to move the runner up or swing away?"

Amanda shrugged and then said, "Look at that. His costume is dirty."

"Well, we call it a uniform, not a costume."

"I'm talking about the mascot."

Oh.

As the runner was cut down trying to steal second and the Mustangs galloped off the field, the Braves' mascot, who was dressed in a toga, engaged in mock combat with the visiting team's "chicken." But that wasn't the only attraction. Mr. Trash was introduced and he turned out to be a young man with an open black garbage bag. We sang "YMCA". They had a "Guess the Attendance" contest. (No fair trying to count), a Loudest Fan contest, a Dirtiest Car in the Parking Lot contest and lots of other distractions.

Between innings, two kids came out of the stands, put their respective foreheads on bats and then tried to run the bases. The beer vendor came by a few times. He was dressed in a Pantera T-shirt and sported a modified Mohawk haircut. The announcer introduced two celebrities, "Mr. and Mrs. George Bush," and a couple who put up with this joke just about every home game took a bow.

We left in the seventh inning with the home team comfortably ahead 15-6, bought a hot dog on the way out and heard the lusty strains of "Take Me Out to the Ball Game," as we got to our rental car. And then we got lost again. Finally, after seeing an ominous sign that read, "Welcome to Idaho Falls," we were able to find our way back to our starting point in time to see the news report of the game.

The sports guy didn't have much film of the Braves' victory so he showed a clip from the previous night's contest in which the manager, Don Werner, argued a third strike call and the umpire ejected him from the game.

Why? Well, first of all, he got down into the catcher's crouch to show the man in blue where the pitch was caught. Then he dropped to his knees and begged him to get it right the next time. After tearing his lineup card into confetti and throwing it into the air, Werner scooped up the scraps and buried them at home plate. Then he crawled on his knees and elbows and pretended to toss a hand grenade at the pitcher's mound.

Amanda smiled. "Let me tell you what the kids behind us said..."

We left Idaho that summer with warm memories of "Old Faithful," the geyser, minor league baseball, potatoes and Jackson Hole, Wyoming. So what is it about Idaho?

The last time we were there, it was just Anna and I. My older brother Tom had suddenly died of a heart attack and we flew to Boise to visit Leeann, his widow, and the rest of the family. Tom's grandson Parker had been in the house when it happened and only a month or so had passed since then. As far as I could tell, he was dealing with the tragedy pretty well for a boy of about ten years.

We were sitting in the living room. I had plopped myself down in a corner chair and was, as I often do, expounding on some subject. My audience seemed to be drifting off in thought, but Parker was transfixed. Encouraged, I delved more deeply into my material. Then Parker bolted up and ran from the room.

Leeann went after him and then came back. "You looked so much like your brother just then," she said.

About a year previously, we drove up there to pick up my Dad, who'd been visiting for about a month, and bring him back to Madera.

I recall Tom driving us all up to the town of McCall, which was about two hours drive north of his home in Caldwell. We had been invited to a local family's house for lunch and they served us elk.

No, I'm not going to rail against hunting. People seem to enjoy it and who am I to deny them that pleasure especially when I'm eating the meat. But the hunter couldn't keep from telling us how he'd spotted the elk on a hillside, serenely scanning the valley below and how the animal had raised his head, paused as if to take in the glorious day.

And then the gunshot and the elk fell. That's how fast it can happen.

After our day at the beach, when we all decided it was time to head inland and prepare for dinner. That's when I was confronted by Rolando, a likeable young man, who invited me to go with him to an office where all of the benefits of a time-share could be fully explained.

Of course, I had been warned. Priti advised me not to speak Spanish at all and thus make it that much more difficult to present the sales pitch. But I ignored that suggestion.

"They will not give up until they take you over there," she told me. "It isn't so much the ones who are out here searching for customers but the sales people back in the office. The guys like Rolando, the one we met right as we checked in, have to bring in every warm body because they believe a certain percentage won't be able to resist."

To me, that didn't make sense. How much more efficient it would be to single out only those who were legitimate prospects and concentrate on them.

"Believe me," she said, "they've been at this a long time. They know what they're doing. And they are more persistent than you are." The glances around the group told me that I'd either just been paid a great compliment or been jabbed a little.

"Sorry," added Priti, clarifying which.

So, as Anna, Priti and Missy enjoyed a late afternoon coffee under a gazebo and the couple from Idaho tended to some undisclosed "packing" back in their room, I was an easy target for Rolando.

He was shocked when I agreed to be taken to the office. Rolando passed me off to an older man, whose name I do not remember because, from the very beginning of our conversation, I had decided to adopt an entirely different identity. For the purposes of this face to face, I would essentially be Loren Eiseley.

Until I found a copy of the book, "Nebraska Moments," in the library the previous month, I had never even heard of this man born in 1907 in Lincoln.

"I was a solitary child in a divided household," he once wrote. "I never saw my mother weep. It was her gift to make others suffer instead." He discounted his father's misfortunes as "bad luck."

Impoverished and reclusive, Loren spent most of his time, as a friend said, "in the intimate company of the contents of abandoned houses, woods, fields and stream edges."

He didn't finish high school but was allowed to enroll at the University of Nebraska in 1925. He'd spent most of his youth reading so writing came naturally to him. One of his teachers glanced at one of his first essay assignments and rejected it outright. "You didn't compose this," he proclaimed. "It is too well written."

The Great Depression interrupted his studies and Eiseley ended up hopping trains and living in hobo jungles. He contracted tuberculosis, from which he recovered and then, in 1933, finally graduated from college with a degree in English and Anthropology.

He ended up teaching at the University of Pennsylvania, where, in 1957, he published his first book, *The Immense Journey,* which has been translated into ten languages and sold more than 500,000 copies. He followed that, in 1958, with *Darwin's Century,* which earned him more acclaim. His autobiography, *All The Strange Hours: The Excavation of A Life,* is described as "haunting." The title refers to Eiseley's lifelong struggle with insomnia and that he used those dark interludes to write most of his works.

Even when things got better for Eiseley and his wife, he never forgot the abject poverty of his youth. The couple never owned a house and gave away their 1939 Dodge in 1966 when he became ill. He died in 1977.

Eiseley enjoyed telling one particular story. A man walking along the ocean spotted a youngster who was picking up star fish and throwing them back into the sea.

When the man asked about this odd behavior, the youngster said that, if he didn't help out the creatures, they would dry up on the beach and die. The older man pointed out that there were thousands of star fish on the beach and miles and miles of sand. "What you're doing," he said, "won't make a bit of difference." The boy shrugged, picked up another star fish and, hurling it into the surf, replied, "It will to that one."

Of course, I had to edit my tale for the occasion, updating it to more modern times, and, in my version, my major was Spanish with a minor in Anthropology. As for the books, I couldn't use his, so I substituted the three I'd written.

This was the only part of my tale that had some truth to it. "Well, to be honest," I told the shocked salesman, "I've sold 12 so far. That's 12 total. Between three books. Not 12 each."

"Actually, this trip is a once-in-a-lifetime event. The university will let us stay in the house, but I won't be required to teach any classes. In fact, they prefer I don't talk to the students very much at all."

"Please don't tell my wife or friends about this," I begged. "They don't know yet. Let's give Anna this one week of peace and relaxation before... well... tragically, the end."

Believing that I had both eliminated myself as a prospect and yet endeared myself to the sales force, I shook hands as I left. Rolando was not waiting for me. He must have been trolling for fresh meat.

There was a golf cart right outside the office but no one offered to give me a ride so I walked back to our room, let myself in and took a nap.

Every since she was a baby, Priti had been exactly that... pretty. Her parents and siblings reached the point where they had to pause to remember the name on her birth certificate but at least they knew what it was. To everybody else who came into her life, she was Priti (the phonetic spelling just seems more exotic to me).

She hadn't come to this island alone. There was a husband at first but after a few years, the postcards and letters sent back to California omitted any mention of him. Maybe that sounds casual, an afterthought, but it was terrible, a tragedy, an unexpected, cruel punch in the stomach for Priti, but she did not share that pain with us.

Missy, single and free to go wherever she chose, rushed to visit her childhood friend with the intention of staying just a few weeks, maybe a month. That was five years ago.

They were very much alike and yet so different. Priti was tall, blonde, artistic and, to some extent, regal. I wouldn't go so far as to say she was a proud woman, just confident, self-assured and energetic.

Missy, short for Mary Elizabeth, had dark hair, was of smaller stature, a practical person who was content with the basics when it came to material things but extended herself greatly for her faith and her friends.

They each had a small apartment, the ones I'd explored back in Santiago, but, from time to time, they would make Missy's available so visitors could stay with them. The previous week, there had been a full house, with Anna, Priti and Missy on one side and Jerry and Linda on the other.

Anna told me, when we were lolling on the beach, that I should expect a steady stream of people coming up the stairs to the veranda. "First, there's Priti's art students and then Missy teaches English over the Internet but some come in person. Besides that, they have friends who pop in all the time. It seems as if the whole city takes turns coming by to see them."

A major source of that foot traffic was, of course, the congregation of Jehovah's Witnesses, one of the 40 or so that operate in Santiago.

When Priti developed a serious medical condition, for example, and her insurance coverage had lapsed, so how was she to get any kind of health care? It turned out there was a woman in the congregation who was a doctor, a general practitioner and she knew another woman, a surgeon, who performed this operation.

After the surgery, Priti was literally carried by her "brothers" up the stairs to her second-story apartment where she convalesced and grew stronger.

"We lack for nothing," she told me.

Our quick shuttle bus ride from the main residential buildings of the resort to an Italian restaurant nearby had reminded me that not everyone adapts as well as Missy and Priti.

We boarded the bus to the sound of a New York accent, a woman complaining loudly about every single detail of her stay. The griping was directed toward three children we assumed were hers, because of the way in which they played their roles in this comedy. "Now kids, please tell me that those windows are open. No? Is there air conditioning? I can't feel any air conditioning. They have vents, but there's nothing come out of them. What a joke! Be careful when these people pass. We wouldn't anyone falling onto the filthy floor. Don't touch anything! How dirty!"

The driver bore it all without a word, just continued to announce the stops. Yes, it was hard to understand his English but all one had to do was look out the window and see if it was the destination.

"What is that man saying kids? Is that supposed to be English? Geez! I have no idea what he's trying to say."

At some point, another passenger leaned over and pointed. Based on having listened to the entire tirade from the very beginning, the fellow traveler knew this was where New York Lady wanted to get off.

She rose and beckoned her children to do the same. Spontaneous applause rippled through the shuttle bus and the woman turned and crowed, "I feel sorry for you guys. You have to stay on the bus." Our pity went out to the waiters at the restaurant she'd chosen that night.

We had no reservations at the Italian restaurant, so the waiters brought out a table and some chairs and set us up on a patio a few steps away from a fountain that gurgled in such a way that it sounded like a bouncy melody. Our party of six did not dine alone, however. There was a cat patrolling the area and she did quite well with this group. The waiter thought we were shooing it away and, between courses, we heard a splash. The cat sprang out of the fountain and ran off toward some bushes where she would recuperate and then return in time for flan a la mode.

Our after-dinner stroll took us to the stage production, "Collage," in which the "Animation Team," which spent all day leading guests in their swimming pool exercises and playing recorded tropical tunes all day, donned colorful costumes and put on a show.

Their energy overwhelmed the audience. If they are somewhat lacking in technique, who cared? If they weren't completely synchronized as they whipped their bodies around in a frenzy, who would notice? Not I.

The master of ceremonies laid down the plot line, a primer on Dominican folklore, but the audience hadn't come to see a history lesson. Before the actual show began, however, some resort guests apparently felt free to let their children, some of them toddlers, climb up on the stage and the steps leading up to an upper level. When the curtain went up, revealing a young stocky man dressed as a Dominican chieftain, he was not alone on stage.

A woman and her two-year-old in clear sight were apparently unaware that the audience participation part of the program was at the end of the production, not the beginning. The "cacique" did his best to coax the two of them off the stage without betraying any irritation for this intrusion and most of the audience played along.

Not Anna. She let out a lusty boo and said as loudly as possible that this was the kind of behavior that should not be tolerated.

The best part came when volunteers were invited up from the audience to contend for the Chief's Crown and the hand of the princess. As a lark, I was about to indicate my willingness to compete, but Priti gave me a stern look and said, "Take my advice. This isn't something you want to do. Wait and you'll see what I mean."

In due time, there were five men on stage and they were asked to imitate the dance moves demonstrated by young men dressed in loin cloths. Each of these "steps" progressively became more suggestive until one young lad bolted from the stage. The chief sent warriors after the fugitive and they made a production out of being frustrated by his escape. Oh how deliciously low!

I looked over at Priti and mouthed, "Thank you."

The "winner" turned out to be a short, pudgy man with boundless energy, a genuine good sport, who somehow made even the most salacious part of the performance into pure innocent fun.

After breakfast the next morning, we walked over to the main building to take a tour of the city of Puerto Plata.

Jose, our tour guide, had black hair, skin to match, a jovial spirit but, underneath it all, tight control on everything that happened during our tour.

When we boarded, the bus, there was a Peruvian man and his New Hampshire wife, both in their twenties, who managed a restaurant in Washington, D.C. and a Guatemalteco and his wife, who was born in South Korea, and they hailed from San Francisco, Calif.

We were driven to a cable car that scaled a mile high mountain called Mt. Isabel de Torres. At the top there was a concrete Christ, his arms spread wide just like the one in Rio de Janeiro in Brazil. While we waited for our turn to be lifted up to view the city, a sleight of hand artist entertained us with card tricks. Not everyone was thrilled with the prospect of being suspended in midair but, as promised by Jose, it all went off without a hitch. Young men offered to take photographs of us in poses that would make it look as if we were in the palm of Christ's hand.

Our next stop was the Brugal rum factory, where we watched the bottling process. After that, the bus took us to the city's center, where we were let loose to buy souvenirs. As we were being led from one store to another, the driver, Tito, was surprised to see his young daughter who'd finished her studies at school and was walking with a group of her friends.

They two of them greeted each other just as I did my girls when they were let out of school. Funny how much alike we are no matter where we might be on this planet.

Both of my girls were born in Los Banos, California, a breezy little town on the west side of the San Joaquin Valley. Less than an hour away, toward the coast, there is a place called Casa de Fruta, which started out as a fruit and vegetable stand and has grown into this charming destination. There's a Casa de Vino, a Casa de Candy, and an outcasa, if you get my joke.

The Disney Channel had been launched on cable and our children fell victim to it and started a daily campaign to get us to take them down to Anaheim and visit "the happiest place on earth."

My newspaper career wasn't going so well at that time so I began delivering the Fresno Bee as well as editing the Los Banos Enterprise. Ethical questions aside, I had a grueling schedule that gave me not a single day off.

So one Sunday afternoon, when we'd heard enough on the subject of the Magic Kingdom, I said, "Well, let's go right now."

And we drove up to Casa de Fruta and told them it was Disneyland.

Because they were so young or wise beyond their years, Anisa and Amanda enjoyed it immensely. After all, there's a railroad with cars just big enough for children, a white buffalo, ducks and geese, maybe some other barnyard animals, along with good hamburgers and French fries.

We played this same trick on them when we drove them to Storyland at Roeding Park in Fresno. The younger one said it looked different from the first time. Anisa must have known what was going on because she reassured her sister, "Oh yes, they've made a lot of changes."

When we finally owned up to our subterfuge and actually took them all the way to Anaheim to the real Disneyland, believe it or not, both of them were disappointed. Amanda recoiled at all the rides except, "It's A Small World," and Anisa was irritated that we didn't buy an umbrella, as she continuously urged us to do.

Late that afternoon, a rare thunderstorm swept through Southern California and, for the first time in decades, the park had to be closed. And all the umbrellas were gone.

We lived close enough to a school to walk our children there and back and, later on, we drove them to and from their high school. All that came back to me when I saw the tour bus driver and his daughter.

"This country's economy runs on tips," Jose told us as we drove back to the resort. "Wages are low so just about everyone has a place to go in the morning. The cost of living here depends on how you want to live."

I had noticed that even before Jose brought it to our attention. At the resort, this same "cheap labor" policy was evident. There's a whole group of young men and women who are part of the "Animation Staff." The word, we decided, was a clumsy translation from the Spanish concept of "encouragement or livening up". These were the performers in the stage show who, during the day, led the guests in mid-morning and mid-afternoon exercise programs. Imagine how many more employees worked in other essential services like housekeeping, gardening, food preparation.

Later, when we returned to Santiago, I saw further evidence. At a supermarket, for example, turn a corner with a grocery cart and three young women standing in an aisle offer to find any item. At the checkout stand, a small army of young men are right there, ready to take purchases out to the car or taxi stand. A nominal wage paid by the store was obviously supplemented by tips.

Out in the parking lot, two or three men carrying sawed-off shotguns kept watch on the customer's vehicles. These "watcheemen" as they were called were quite an unnerving sight at first, but, in no time at all became part of the landscape. The larger stores had towers from which the guards watched over the clientele. But I never saw anyone detained nor was there even a hint of disorder or a fracas of any kind. Maybe it all happened when we were safely back in our rooms either at the resort or El Ensueno, but we never were witness to it.

Something else I never saw, although others might have, is any evidence of the senseless gang activity that plagues the United States. Tattoos might adorn a Dominican body, but I couldn't say for sure because they were either covered by clothing or don't exist.

Speaking of clothing, the only men who wear shorts are tourists. The Dominican man prefers a pair of pants that, in spite of the heat, covers his lower limbs. Maybe inside his home at this very moment, the average adult Dominican male could be stretching out in a comfortable pair of shorts, but I didn't see that either.

When I went to a large warehouse type hardware store, a Home Depot type place, the system employed to check out customers required the maximum amount of staff. At the entrance to the parking lot, we had to stop and take a paper authorizing us to drive in.

Once inside, we were approached immediately, asked what we might be looking for and then led to that part of the enormous store. When we found the item, we did not grab it and take it with us to the cashier. We pointed it out for the clerk who filled out a receipt, which we took to the front of the store. The cashier accepted payment and then the materials were delivered into our hands or to our car, if that's what we preferred.

This is why, in my opinion, there was never any group of unemployed young men gathered on a street corner or loitering in a strip mall parking lot. Those not hired were self-employed, selling something or performing some service.

There was a man who set up a small table with a coffee pot, connected by a cable to a battery, and brewed individual cups of a hot, black brew for passersby and those waiting for the next bus. In the cool early spring mornings, it seemed to be a jolly way to make a living, but I knew that, during the long hot months when the humidity sapped one's strength, that coffee salesman and others like him would scrape by with the sweat of their brow.

The Dominican method might seem strange to us, but I couldn't come up with a better alternative.

Jose had the driver take us by the mayor's house in Puerto Plata. He made no comment other than identifying it, leaving us to supply the, "Pretty nice. Impressive. Wonder how much that cost?"

Our dinner companions that night included two couples from the province of Ontario in Canada. They explained  why so many of their countrymen were "snowbirds," semi-permanent fixtures at these Dominican resorts.

"It costs so much to heat a house during our winters," said a portly man with a completely bald head and a prodigious mustache, "that we can pay for most of this trip with the money we save from not having to buy heating oil."

"We can't just let the house freeze," his wife, a hardy woman with frizzy gray hair, said. "If the pipes freeze, then it's possible we'd have a break in the water line and then, watch out, the place would flood and then freeze over. We'd be going back to an ice cave."

"So you hire a house tender, someone to stop by and check on your property, right?" I suggested and started plotting out an entire story built around this lonely figure going from one empty upper class home to another.

"We have relatives who go by and check on our house, but I guess, if someone didn't have any family, they might do that," the husband said.

Too late. I already envisioned him, this young man, Henri by name, who trudged through snow knee-deep on his way to inspect yet another home on his route of, well let's say, a dozen houses.

My imagination gave way to my memory, however, as I thought about one of our first trips together as a married couple. There is a park up in the San Francisco Bay Area where people can enjoy a touch of Africa as well as the earth's oceans. It's called Marine World or something like that and the whole illusion is done with live animals and aquariums, along with attractions and shows and we decided one weekend to drive up there.

It took us about three hours to reach our destination and when we pulled into the parking lot, I suspected something was wrong because there were so few vehicles there. The place, we soon realized, was closed because the owners were in the process of moving to another location even farther from Madera.

My mother-in-law posed in front of the big sign and we took the picture, got back in our little Volkswagen bug and wandered around San Francisco. To this day, we laugh about that weekend.

The real traveler in our family is, of course, Anna. Even before I met her, in spite of the age of her parents, they were not afraid to light out of Manhattan and head for the country.

After her father died, Anna and her mother went to a convention of Jehovah's Witnesses in Washington D.C. and, when I heard that story, all I could think was, "That wouldn't happen in my family."

Anna and her mother, who would have been in her 60's at that time, went on the bus to the nation's capital and then took a taxi to the house where lodgings had been secured. At that time, the congregations at the host city would go out and seek rooms at little cost for the out-of-town delegates. Sometimes, the houses weren't in the nicest of neighborhoods.

When Anna and her mother tried to return that night after the evening session, they boarded the wrong bus, ended up in an even more dangerous area, far from where they should have been. In the darkness, they could see one street lamp and gathered underneath it, a few unsavory characters. They were finally able to hail a taxi, which took them back to where they were staying.

When I heard that story, I marveled. "We wouldn't have even gone," I said.

My future bride and her mother were more shocked about that than I was about the perils of Washington D.C.

In the summer of our first year married, the three of us took off for our convention in Los Angeles, at the Fabulous Forum, and halfway there, on Highway 99 somewhere beyond Bakersfield, the VW suddenly coughed, choked and stalled. I sat there for a moment, with absolutely no idea what to do, and then I got out.

"Where are you going?" Anna asked.

I did not resent the implication that I was not going to fix the problem because I made no secret of my ignorance of mechanical things.

"I'll be right back," I assured my young wife.

I went back to the rear-engine vehicle, opened up the hood and looked directly at the motor. "Please let us get to Los Angeles," I pleaded quietly. "Just to L.A. and back to Madera. After that, you can just sit there and do nothing. Never have to run again. OK?"

Then I got back behind the wheel, turned the key and the car came back to life.

Anna looked at me as if I'd just made the Empire State Building disappear. "What did you do?"

"Oh it was nothing," I shrugged. "Just vapor lock," an expression I'd heard but had not the slightest idea of its meaning.

That Volkswagen got us to our rooms, kindly given to us by a lady of our faith, and then we made it to every one of the five days of our convention. The only thing was we had to push the car to start it every time. But that's part of owning a VW, isn't it?

We drove back to Madera, parked the little car outside the kitchen window and it never ran again.

Our final morning of all-inclusive resort relaxation meant that it was time to say goodbye to Jerry and Linda. A shuttle bus would take them to the airport for a flight back to Idaho and then the rest of us would be dropped off at the bus station.

The driver extended us one last courtesy by loading our luggage for us but, once we were back at the bus station and we had thanked him with a tip, we went back to being middle class tourists on a rare visit to paradise.

Instead of getting on the bus to Santiago, we were ushered into Danny's unmarked taxi. We made a brief stop at Cabarete, a strip of beach which seems to have escaped the voracious appetite of the tourist industry. Regular folks can lay down a towel and sun bathe up away from the surf if they want to. Back at the resort, the locals were confined to a tiny strip of sand, usually wet, right along the shore.

Danny must have snickered at us as we were immediately targeted by the beggars who patrol the parking lot. We followed his lead and simply ignored them.

I was struck by the fact that no one seemed concerned about their property left lying on towels in the sand while its owners splashed in the surf. There appeared to be some kind of code that prevented the beggars from becoming thieves.

But what was troubling was the stray dog going, it seemed, from tiny campsite to tiny campsite, sniffing and peeing in any open purse or bag.

The road from the beach to Santiago revealed in all of its heartbreaking reality the face of poverty in the Dominican Republic. Large families stood in front of structures that didn't appear to be fit for livestock. Children rushed out from the medians with flowers in their hands, begging motorists who stopped for a traffic signal to purchase a bunch for whatever few coins might be handy.

We saw a truck loaded with milpa, a grain that looks like wheat, ahead of us and, suddenly, a man popped up in the middle of it.

We passed an abandoned restaurant, a failure in spite of the clever sign that read, "If your wife can't cook, don't divorce her. Bring her here!" I offered my opinion that this was the principal reason the place was no longer in business. What wife would be amused if her husband took her there?

7

The Veranda at El Ensueno

We arrived back at El Ensueno to find Eugenia Robles Guadarama, whom everyone called Gladys, rushing around preparing a meal for us.

Gladys was as dark as I am pale, about 30 years younger and about an inch taller than me. There is no doubt that, somewhere along the line, she had Haitian ancestors, but her language was Spanish and her nationality, Dominican. But none of that really describes her. What identifies Gladys is her love of God and neighbor.

Although she cleaned other people's houses to make a living, Gladys concentrates on teaching others the Bible at least 70 hours a month, the same as Missy and Priti.

Later on, in conversation with Gladys, I found out that she wanted to attend a school for those who have agreed to set this goal but, for one reason or another, hadn't been invited. Gladys let it be known that, should an opening in a class come up, she'd drop everything to enroll for the two-week course.

That call came three years after she began her intensive door to door ministry and, wouldn't you know it, at one of the most inconvenient times. She had been hired as a bookkeeper at "The Palace," the local city hall, but didn't have any sick time or vacation time saved up. I am only assuming that such an arrangement even existed there.

But she'd made a vow. Not only would she put in those 70 hours, but attend that school no matter when the invitation came. So she left her job and went for the two weeks instruction.

From the way she told the story, I did not ask if she had any regrets. My circle of acquaintances on the island was obviously small, but in that group, I never met anyone happier than Gladys. She had recently accepted an invitation to move to a small rural town, San Juan de Afuera, which means St. John Outside, beyond the city limits.

"A man who owns a store heard we (meaning herself and another young woman just as determined to spread God's word) needed a place to live and so he built us one."

It wasn't much more than large box made of concrete with a metal roof, but soon friends back in Santiago filled it with furniture and other amenities. The two ladies couldn't have been more content.

In a moment of bravura, I invited Gladys to a one-on-one game of dominos. She obliged and complimented me several times on a few good moves before summarily dispatching me as an opponent.

It is a simple game really. One "ficha" after another until they are all gone. First one to do so, wins. But at the same time, so much strategy.

I learned to play dominos at work, in the Madera County Courthouse when my interpreting skills were not needed at that particular moment. There were four of us gathered around a metal table that had been minding its own business sitting against a wall when I brazenly appropriated it for our office.

The slapping of the dominos on the metal surface gave off what I thought was a delightful sound. In time, I found out that administrative personnel found it quite distracting and unbecoming.

The point is that I really didn't understand the game. My opponents, usually two Mexican-Americans and one young man, half Puerto Rican and half Mexican, were pretty well matched. I, on the other hand, never won.

Once, as I stood outside the door helping a defendant fill out a plea form, I heard one of them say, "Do you think Jim is losing on purpose?" The others laughed.

"I mean," he continued, "the way he plays makes no sense. He knows the rules and understands what we're doing, right?"

That motivated me, one lazy afternoon, to ask the Puerto Rican-Mexican, Moses by name, just what I was doing wrong. "Everything," he replied. "It's like you're playing a completely different game."

When I explained my strategy, he howled and had to catch his breath. When the other players came into the office, he couldn't wait to tell them my "secret plan."

"He wants to keep one of each number so, no matter what we play, he always has a ficha ready. Isn't that crazy?"

So they began to teach me and, when I actually won I jumped to my feet, thrust my hands straight up in the air as if I'd just scored a touchdown, pushed open the office door and paraded down the hallway to the shock of the attorneys and clients who were milling around out there.

As time went on, I added another bit of business. After losing five or six times, if given a good hand and things fell just right and I won, I would yell, "Gotta' go!" and then, up went the arms and out the door I'd go.

Dominicans and Puerto Ricans usually play in pairs, two against two. For some reason, it is of upmost importance to let your partner know which "fichas" you have. I'm told that so much signaling goes on in the constant chatter and subtle gestures that, in high stakes tournaments, the players are actually shielded from one another's sight. Only the pieces are visible. I never saw this but am assured it has to be that way to prevent cheating.

We were joined later on by two men, one very light skinned with blue eyes. He was accompanied by a man about my age who spoke not ten words the whole time we played. It took me several hands to realize this portly dark man was my partner and then, about 30 minutes into the game, something else became apparent. I'd noticed that whenever he played, the others would say, "How kind," which is "Amable," in Spanish. When I joined in, the others half-smiled as what they thought was my play on words. See, Amable was his name.

Gladys and "Blue Eyes" had the advantage because one member of the opposing team, me, failed to follow his partner's lead. Not only didn't I notice which "fichas" Amable played, but wasn't even aware I should have.

A stillness settled over Santiago. The breeze that lifted the clouds up to the hills had calmed, exhausted by the effort. Later, perhaps, the clouds would rise up, clamber up the green mountains and drop a little rain. But, for now, they were in repose.

And so was I.

Up on the terrace, surrounded by palm trees, mango trees and flowers, while the constant breeze cooling me, I was completely content.

A notebook on the table began to fill with what sounded like poetry to me. Later on, far away from El Ensueno, the lines didn't have the same charm. But maybe I'm judging my own work too harshly.

Down on the street level, a child spoke in a tropical rhythm, words jumping off his tongue, rattling the air. The cry I understood as "Mundo," or "The World," caught my attention and I grabbed a few pesos and headed down to buy what I thought would be a newspaper. But it turned out he was saying, "Mondongo," which is a Puerto Rican dish, most tasty, a cup of plaintain filled with a variety of ingredients.

A woman with a tub on her head glided elegantly by and sang that same song I heard on my first morning here. That day, however, she stopped because a customer swooped out of a house and wanted to inspect the fruits and vegetables. Between the two of them, they lowered the tub to the sidewalk and then the negotiations got underway. When the purchase was complete, the vendor squatted slightly and the customer carefully replaced the tub filled with produce squarely on her head. A few steps later, the song began again, "Guandules!"

The sound of buses and conchos created a constant roar, a foggy tumult that rose and subsided, punctuated by roosters crowing. Morning rush hour also seemed to stir up the birds that who chatted away but then retreated to their nests and roosts to endure the heat of the day.

Then there was the sound of two doors slamming, the unlatching of a trunk, the footsteps coming up the stairs to the terrace. Danny appeared first and right behind him, there was Kookie.

Actually her name was Refugio, but the diminutive in Spanish is Cuca, which, if you want to be even more informal, becomes Cuquita (pronounced Kookeeta) and, finally, to an English-speaking ear, Kookie.

And, to be honest, she is, a little bit. Since we'd discussed this in the past, I knew her to be exactly 15 years younger than me. Her appearance varied, from thin to chunky depending on how she felt, and, at that moment, I could tell she was somewhere between stressed and content.

"This is a surprise!" I shouted.

"It's supposed to be," she yelled back. "Where is everybody?"

Everybody had all been inside, busy with making breakfast or setting up their "classes" for that day, but, upon hearing that distinctive Puerto Rican voice, Anna, Missy and Priti all charged out to greet Kookie.

"I heard you were going to be here and decided to catch a plane and horn in on your vacation," said our new arrival. "They knew I was coming."

We clustered around the table and caught up on the latest news from North Carolina, where Kookie now lived with her mother (Mami) along with her recently married sister and husband.

"Silvino are happy, still on the honeymoon," Kookie said and we all understood that it would be her custom to refer to the two people as one and by the husband's last name. "The other day, I walked by their bedroom and they'd left their door open so I got a shock. They were in the middle of some pirouettes and somersaults. I swear he was spinning her around like a plate on a stick."

I almost choked on a pancake.

"The other day, we were driving around and my sister saw a sign, '5 Movies $5,' and she just insisted we should drive around for hours looking for this bargain. We had to go back to the sign and find the address. Then, we drove up and down the streets of Charlotte until, finally, Silvino spotted the place. As we were driving up, I saw that the place sold adult movies, but I kept my beak shut and let them go all the way in. A few seconds later, they came running out... and I mean literally running... with a look in their eyes, like they'd been to Sodom and Gomorrah."

"I guess they weren't interested in learning some new somersaults and pirouettes," I said.

I
t wasn't that many years ago that Kookie and the four of us, Anna, my daughters and I, were driving down Highway 99 going to Fresno, when a cell phone went off.

I was sitting in the back seat, right behind the driver, Anna, and Kookie was in the front passenger seat. From that angle, I saw her answer the phone, bow her head slightly and then begin to cry.

There is an expression in Spanish, "le saltaron las lagrimas," which means literally, "the tears jumped out of her eyes," and that is exactly what happened.

"My Dad just died," said Kookie as Anna pulled our van to the side of the road.

He was back in Caguas, Puerto Rico and it would be impossible for Kookie to fly all the way back there in time so that Saturday we listened to the funeral over the telephone in our living room that Saturday. My memory is that Missy and some of her family also attended. All of us dressed up as if we were at the Kingdom Hall there in Caguas and we looked up the Bible texts and sang the song at the end.

That time we went to Idaho, Kookie was living in the same house as Missy and her sister and we took off one morning from Idaho Falls to Yellowstone National Park. When we got there, expecting "Old Faithful" to spout off every few minutes, we found out that the geyser needs more time than that to recharge itself, so we were all waiting and staring at this natural wonder from the second story of a rustic lodge.

After a few minutes, I had to break in and say, "Sorry, but I've got to go to the bathroom."

"Me too," said Kookie and we went off to our respective facilities.

On our way back to the others, we saw an older man in a wheelchair and, just being friendly, said hello.

"Hello to you two too," he hollered.

I guessed he was losing his hearing.

"Where are you from, dearie?"

Kookie looked him right in the eye. I could tell she suspected he was surprised to see someone like her out there in Wyoming. Kookie's hair is naturally curly, even frizzy, and it takes more than a few minutes to tame it every day. That particular morning, the process wasn't as complete as she might have liked. That, along with her dark complexion, caught this older man's eye and curiosity.

Kookie smiled. "I'm from Hoboken, New Jersey," she chirped.

"Well, God bless America!" the man hollered. "I am too."

And he proceeded to tell us about his living in the same neighborhood as Frank Sinatra and how his mother knew Mrs. Sinatra and they used to wash their clothes together and gossip and how he met Old Blue Eyes a few times and he's not as bad a guy as people sometimes say and...

Well, we missed Old Faithful spouting off a second time. It was only on the third cycle that Kookie and I got to see the eruption. Very impressive.

"I'm going to quit my job," Kookie was saying as I started paying attention to the conversation again. "The other day, I was helping this young girl, pregnant, fill out her forms to get cash aid for the baby. The man was standing behind her and I just didn't like his looks."

I caught on that Kookie had taken employment at the Welfare Department in North Carolina.

"So, when we were finished, I said to the girl, 'There's one more form to fill out. I'll go get it for you. It's the one you need for when the father here abandons you and your child and leaves you with nothing.' The man sneered at me and the girl said, 'Oh no, that's all right. That's not going to happen.'"

"Well, I know it's going to happen," Kookie growled. "I see it every day."

Once, after a long day at the department, Kookie told us, "All day long, I hear about people's problems, how they just lost their job, their husband just left them, they don't have a place to live, no food in the house. See, they just have their story to tell. Just one story. I hear it all day long from dozens of people. I'm the victim around here!"

From then on, whenever Kookie would get started, there was always someone who would pipe up and say, "So who's the victim around here?"

And, right on cue, she'd repeat that line.

Over the years, Kookie's friends had learned to understand her quirky vocabulary.

For example, "noon at night," was midnight.

"A Brazilionaire," was the rich bachelor who won the girl on that reality show a few years ago.

The Tom Hanks movie where he met the girl on top of the Empire State Building? "Speechless in Seattle."

She ordered chicken fried steak and, when it was placed before her, Kookie asked, "How do you get this chicken so dark? It tastes great, but not like any chicken I've ever had." And she wasn't kidding.

"My sister really jumped into it the other day," she said as the five of us went out to the terrace after breakfast.

"Silvino had been watching that old movie, 'Mighty Joe Young,' and it occurred to her to say, 'My, but that gorilla looks just like grandma. Look! Right around the eyes.'"

"So Mami got mad and said, 'Don't you talk about my mother like that! I don't talk about your mother!"

"But Ma, you are my mother!"

"Yes. That's what I say!"

We all laughed but I'm not sure, even now, exactly what we found so funny.

Anna invited Kookie to go with her down the street and around the corner to a hair salon called Kajeebra so they could enjoy a spa day of sorts.

Priti had some art students coming over and Missy would be conducting English classes via the internet, so it wasn't long before I had the terrace to myself.

L ate in the afternoon, the birds suddenly came back to life, yapping and squawking and one, in particular, trilled deep in his throat making a rattling sound.

Could it have been the same bird that slipped through the slats of the shutters and partook of the dog's kibble?

By the wrought iron staircase that led up to the upper reaches of our building, there are two large plastic cans. That is where garbage was deposited and, on some inconsistent schedule, the city's sanitation department dispatched trucks to go out into the streets of Santiago to pick it up. A few times I saw a man amble up the steps, take hold of a can, drag it down to the street, empty it and then repeat the process with the second receptacle.

But there is another method of garbage disposal. Some folks produced prodigious amounts of empty boxes and cans, along with foodstuffs and the peelings from potatoes and other tubers. When the cans would be literally overflowing, an older man would timidly creep up the stairs and indicate without a word that he would be willing to dispose of the trash.

All he asked for in return was a tip. But I had no idea how much would be appropriate. Sensing my confusion, a voice from inside the apartment proposed a number. When I extracted a bill from the pesos still in my pocket, it was about twice as much. How the ladies inside the living room watching television knew I was about to overpay for this service, I have no idea. Or it could have been that they just knew I wouldn't go to the trouble of searching for a smaller denomination?

Therefore, the amount was repeated and this time with a certain firmness. "If you give him more, he will expect it next time and, to be honest, we can't afford that on a regular basis."

That sounded reasonable so I flipped through the bills until I found the right one. The man accepted my offer with a nod. As he pulled the large black bags out of the cans and started to drag them away, I made the mistake of adding, "I wasn't sure how much. Is what I gave you enough?"

And this man, who must have been around my age, lifted his head and said, "If that's all you have, that is enough."

At that moment, I wanted to give him the whole wad of bills that bulged in my pocket, but I was just a visitor and had to rely on the judgment of others.

On another day in another neighborhood, I saw what happened to the bags of garbage hauled away in this fashion. I saw a woman straddling what at first appeared to be an open suitcase. As I got closer, it became clear that she was inspecting a large black bag filled with garbage. Meticulously, she examined the contents for anything of value. Several bags were stacked nearby. I could only guess that the "garbage men" fetched the bags and she was assigned this part of the operation.

Down the street and around the corner, there was a business sector and, one afternoon, Anna and I walked in that direction to get some cash out of a bank's ATM and buy a gigantic ice cream cone. In the light of day, I could see that, between the sidewalk and the asphalt pavement, there were gaps about a foot wide and two feet long. The depth of these openings seemed to be about four feet and there were no signs, no markings, no cones to warn anyone of their presence.

Surely, motorcycles, small cars and people have fallen into these rectangular holes. When I expressed that opinion back at the apartment, Priti assured me that she'd never seen anyone or anything fall into them. "People just know they're there."

An emaciated dog slept in the middle of the sidewalk, apparently wasting away, but, day after day, in that exact same spot, there he was. When I expressed sympathy for this poor animal, Priti nodded her agreement, but added, "That's the very first thing I noticed when I first moved here and it bothered me quite a bit. But I'm sorry to say, it wasn't long before the condition of the people sort of erased my concern for the dogs. As for the cats, well, I never had much use for them."

There was a man sitting on a bench in the shade. His hands were empty. He leaned back, clutching a knee to his chest. He wasn't waiting for anyone or anything, just staring across the street. I had an entire chapter of speculation forming in my head when I realized that he owned the business across the street. It was just a tiny concrete garage, more or less, and he was taking a break from doing nothing over there to do nothing across the street.

I lost interest in the lazy businessman when two cars, bumper to bumper, chugged by. Of all the dangerous things you can do on the road, this is the one most fraught with danger. The second car was pushing the first. That's a scene I had not seen in decades. In fact, a young man in Firebaugh, not far from where we live now, died in an accident that started out just that way, one car pushing another. But that day, on the streets of Santiago, no one perceived any danger in it.

Caribbean drivers seem to test fate fearlessly. When our girls were pre-teens, we took them to Puerto Rico. We saw a truck barrel down a mountainside in the middle of the night and were shocked because the driver neglected to turn on his headlights. "I could never drive here," Anna said. Now, that's scary.

We went there principally to visit an old family friend, Pedro Battle. He and his wife Necty had been the witnesses at our wedding and, only a couple of years later, we were devastated to hear that she had died.

The saddest part of it was the fact that she was quite a bit younger than Pedro, who, at the time of our visit, must have been in his 70's. He met us at the San Juan Airport and got into our rented car and guided us to Corozal, one of the smallest towns on the island. Pedro had a place on the side of a mountain and, looking straight down, through the floor boards, we could see cows grazing underneath the house.

I had an extensive notebook of sights that should be seen in Puerto Rico, ranging from the glowing bay in Ponce to the museums in San Juan and the beaches near Mayaguez. Within a couple of days, I realized that we would not be seeing any of those things. Instead, we spent many treasured hours with Pedro and our girls forged a relationship with him that lasted until his death years later.

We had to go back to San Juan a day before our departure and Anna wanted to see a relative who lived in a condominium. It seemed to be an easy task, but we wandered around for hours.

Finally, I stopped a policeman and asked him for directions to this place. And I swear, this was what he told me. "You go down this road until you come to a store on your right. Don't stop. Keep going. Then you will see a park on your left. Don't stop. Keep going. Farther on, you'll see this palm tree, the tallest one in town. Don't stop. Keep going."

I finally broke in. "Just tell me when I should stop, OK?"

The policeman looked at me coolly and said, "Why don't you just follow me?"

Oh, that would be so much better.

Several turns later, we pulled up in front of the police station. I got out and asked if he had to stop for a second before continuing the guided tour toward Anna's relative's apartment.

"No," he said. "I realize now that I don't know where it is." And off he went with what seemed to me to have been a giggle.

We continued our search and, miraculously, found the condo. By then, my eyes were bleary and my red hair practically pulled out by the roots. The older lady who answered the door took one look at us and asked, "Have any trouble finding me?"

L ike the fringe of hair on a bald man, the clouds on the horizon hovered all around us but there was plenty of blue sky above.

Off in the distance, the ringing of church bells and some kind of melodious music joined together in an urban symphony. Then, at 6 a.m. the workers who were remodeling the house next door arrived and immediately started banging a bucket against a wall and talking as loudly as possible.

Just in case someone's sleep has not been disturbed, the construction crew fired up some kind of machinery that sounded like a swarm of gas-powered insects. A man somewhere toward the center of town bellowed something in such a way that I know I'd never buy whatever he was selling.

In a couple of hours, we would drive away from all of this for the tranquility of a relatively secluded beach. It was already getting warm when we trooped down the stairs and packed ourselves a caravan of three cars headed to "Gilligan's Island," the name assigned to our destination.

On the way, I saw a large sports utility vehicle being refueled as a fruit cart was pushed up into a parking lot. And then there was an orange bridge, a miniature Golden Gate, which spanned a dying river filled with garbage. We passed an enormous landfill with mountains of smoldering garbage.

Meanwhile, in the back seat of our car, two of the younger members of our party actually debated the question of Batman and Robin's specific powers.

The streets of Santiago swarmed with vendors. As our caravan paused at an intersection, a man began soaping the windshield. The Chihuahua called Candy launched herself from Priti's arms and yapped furiously. Just as the poor windshield washer was about to exact a small pittance for his labor, a coconut vendor squirmed forward and took his spot at the driver's window. An argument ensued and I can only guess how it escalated when the light changed to green and our driver tromped on the gas and left both of them reeling.

I was stumped later on by a sign that read, in Spanish, "The kiss of the turkey."

We reached the funky little beach where an Austrian man, tanned to a deep golden brown by years of soaking up the Dominican sun, set up his own little kingdom. His castle was a makeshift open air restaurant, actually a series of picnic tables. Fish were taken out of the ocean and chickens out of cages stacked next to the wooden structure where the cooks were hard at work.

There was a toilet but I couldn't see any provision made for drainage so whatever the patrons deposited in there must have been hauled away at some point. Otherwise, well...

We set up our camp, setting down our towels, ice chests, snacks and numerous bottles of sunscreen on the beach chairs provided to us by the Austrian. This jovial beachcomber-businessman counted out how many of us wanted chicken and how many preferred fish and then assured us he'd be back to let us know when our lunch was ready.

Dressed only in swim trunks, he took a few steps and then turned around with the ominous announcement, "Oh by the way. Be careful today. The tide is pretty strong. Don't try to swim. Stay close to the shore. Sorry, but that's the way it is today."

I hadn't planned on actually swimming anyway and, with that warning, neither was anyone else.

Our host told me later on that he'd been in the Dominican Republic for 14 years... no 17 years... well, maybe 14. He couldn't quite remember. "I traveled all over the world before settling down here. I love it. Wouldn't live anywhere else." But I never got a clue as to where exactly he lived, whether in the "kitchen" or a condominium down the road.

Lunch came quickly because we spent what was left of the morning playing dominos, beach badminton and occasionally dipping our toes into the pounding surf. It was a challenge to differentiate the chicken from the fish because both had been prepared in such a way that they looked mummified. But presentation isn't as important as they say. Both dishes were delicious.

A group of Europeans who'd been summering at the Austrian's beach for quite a while, judging by the dark golden tans, played a game in which they rolled wooden balls in the sand. The rules were incomprehensible for us but we enjoyed their competitive spirit.

They were still playing when we packed up our belongings and began our return trip to Santiago.

During my frequent mid-afternoon naps in the back bedroom, I eavesdropped on the family living behind us and kept up with the progress, or lack of it, in the education of a youngster down there. He was not doing well, I gathered. He had no idea of the geography of South America and this had a woman living in the same house quite perturbed. She expressed herself very clearly for about an hour one morning before sending him off to school to try and catch up on his studies.

Besides the shouting between the student and his mother (I assumed that's who she was), another source of constant noise was the water dripping from the tinaco on the roof of the house being renovated next door. Where this water went was a mystery to me but I knew wherever it was, mosquitoes were breeding. But none of them were humming around our bedroom so I dozed peacefully.

My usual table on the terrace was available so I was able to hear very clearly the bleating of a new vendor. "Llevo coco! Llevo los cocos, los cocos. El coquero!" (I have coconuts. I have coconuts, the coconuts. The coconut man!)

I went to the three-foot high banister at the edge of the patio and saw, out in the street, a man pushing a combination wheelchair and baby buggy. Inside this contraption was a pile of green coconuts, just as advertised. Upon closer inspection, I could see that his cart had two big wheels in the back and two smaller ones in the front so that, when he set it down, the "Coquero" presented his produce in its most attractive light.

He moved on, belting out his one hit, and my attention shifted to Gladys, who came out of the apartment with a load of wet laundry in a basket. She climbed the iron staircase to the very top level of the building and began hanging clothes on the wire lines.

The wind was so strong that she had to use three or four pins on each item. Even so, a furious gust snatched a pair of pants from her and sent them sailing over to the roof of the neighboring house. Unfortunately, this was not the neighbor who was in the midst of remodeling. If it had been, then it would have been simple. That building is almost exactly as high as ours. But the wind had carried the clothes in the other direction and that roof was several feet lower.

We were too high to jump down and fetch the pants. Of course, we could have gone downstairs, knocked on our neighbor's door and asked to be allowed access to the roof and retrieved them that way. Gladys shook her head. "This has happened too many times before. I'd rather try and get them ourselves."

Gladys thought about it a while and then said, "I know. We can go to the washroom and, if we had a pole or something, pick the pants up with it."

Coincidentally (or not), there were several long pieces of plastic pipe, the kind used to connect a water tank to the plumbing system or, in the U.S., for sprinkler systems. In just a few minutes, Gladys and I manipulated the PVC pipe through the iron bars on the window, out and down to the pants, hooking them and then carefully pulled them back inside. A great shout of joy, "We did it!"

I celebrated with a Presidente while Gladys returned to the task of washing clothes, carrying clothes, hanging clothes, taking clothes down from the line and refusing my every offer to help.

At some point, I must have returned to our room to take a little nap because, as the wind finally started to calm, I heard a familiar voice.

"He can't speak Spanish and he can't read English so he doesn't understand the teacher here and wasn't doing well in New York, so what am I going to do?" the lady wailed.

The slender lad of about 12 years of age slumped in a chair, totally absorbed by something in the palm of his hand. The woman turned out to be his grandmother, unless raising this kid had aged her prematurely. By walking out of the bedroom and into the living room, I had interrupted the recitation of her grandson's faults, so the least I could do was invite the boy out to the patio for a glass of juice or something.

Without a word, he responded to my wave and we both sought refuge from his grandmother.

Just making small talk, I told Pedro Martinez (obviously named in honor of the future Hall-of-Famer) that there was an interesting story in that day's paper. "They had a protest in Miraflores you know."

Pedro nodded.

"There is a photograph of this crowd of people blocking the streets to make the point that there are too many street vendors and minibuses blocking the streets. How's that for irony, huh?"

Pedro shrugged.

"And today is the International Day of Women."

Pedro sighed.

"Got some interesting stories on outstanding women in the kitchen sharing their experiences, the challenges facing Dominican women and females in the military."

Pedro stared at me with intense disinterest.

"You must be a pitcher," I said in one last attempt at conversation.

"Catcher."

"Good hitter?"

"Not bad."

"Do you play somewhere around here," and I indicated the world beyond the patio.

"There's a field out that way. I hit a homerun there."

"Tell me about it."

And he did, in great detail. The exact location of the pitch, the swing he put on the ball, the arc as it sailed into straight-away center field, how it cleared the yellow tape they'd strung up between the trees to indicate a homerun.

"Felt good, didn't it?"

Pedro Martinez smiled and relived the moment, the fact that his team had been behind and its chances had dimmed with the receding light of early evening. In a flourish, he also provided some background on the rivalry between the two teams from adjacent neighborhoods. If the subject already hadn't been covered by the movie, "The Sandlot," Pedro had the makings of an excellent plot for a film.

"This time of year," I told him, "my Dad and his friends would go down to Arizona for spring training. They wouldn't actually watch any games..."

Missy and grandmother came through the door and I really couldn't tell if the tutoring offer had been accepted or not. Pedro lowered his head, rediscovered the mobile device in his hand and was lost to us again.

As he followed his grandmother down the stairs, I said, "Hope to see you soon Pedro. Maybe talk some baseball." He grunted and shuffled down to the street.

My thoughts were still on baseball and fathers after we ate dinner on the terrace. "My Dad and his buddies went on that spring training trip every year for about 15 years," I said after telling Kookie and Anna about Pedro Martinez.

"When I asked him what they did down there in the desert, Dad said, 'Nothing. Sit in the stands, right in the front row and watch them practice.'"

"They watched the games too, right?" asked Kookie.

"No, that was the oddest thing. They watched the team take infield, that's when the coach bats the ball to each fielder. It's a real ritual. Then there's batting practice. There would only be about 50 people in the stands and they could hear the chatter and ribbing that goes on between ballplayers. That's the sort of thing they'd go see."

"My Dad went to baseball games at Yankee Stadium," Anna said. "This was back when men wore suits to the ball game. We have a picture of him in the bleachers and he's in this large group, all men, all with black suits and white shirts and dark ties."

"My Dad decided to like the Mets," Kookie said. "I don't remember which team he rooted for, the Giants or Dodgers, before they left for California. But I know he wasn't a Yankee fan."

"We would watch the Game of the Week on Saturday afternoons sometimes," Anna said. "And when they'd play the National Anthem, my dad would tell me, 'Stand up! That's your country!' He was born when Puerto Rico was part of Spain and then, later, after the Spanish-American War, the Jones Act made all Puerto Ricans United States citizens. He was proud of that."

I had some baseball stories about my Dad. Plenty of them, in fact, but Kookie had withdrawn into her own thoughts.

It was Missy who lightened the mood.

"Remember Lorenzo the Parrot?"

For a while, Kookie lived with Missy, her mother and her little brother and they had this big white parrot in a cage right outside Kookie's bedroom window.

"That bird would screech and scream for no reason at all," said Kookie. "It would scare me to death."

"It wasn't actually my bird," said Missy. "My mother had it for years. And one day, I came home from work and Mom was all upset about Lorenzo, that he'd fainted. Well, I took one look at the poor thing and realized he'd just died."

"But my Mom insisted he was still breathing a little and wanted me to give it mouth to mouth resuscitation and do CPR on it."

And then Missy bent over the table on the patio and demonstrated how she rhythmically pressed on the bird's chest and then bent over to blow into its open beak. "I kept this up my entire lunch hour, but then it was time to go back to work. So I told my Mom, 'Sorry Ma, Lorenzo didn't make it.'"

That afternoon the grief-stricken woman took the bird, wrapped it in a plastic bag and stuffed it into the freezer. Later, when Kookie opened the refrigerator door to get something to thaw out for dinner, Lorenzo slid out and rattled to the floor.

"Oh, that's Lorenzo," said Missy's Mom. "I was thinking we could maybe get him stuffed. He was such a good bird. I wonder what happened to him."

And that's when all eyes slowly moved to Kookie who smiled and shook her head. "Don't try to pin this on me," she said.

8

As The Sun Sinks Slowly

In comparison to Santo Domingo, the capital city of the republic, Santiago is a tranquil, staid, boring little community.

We dared not drive ourselves, but took the luxury bus again and hired a mini-van taxi to chauffer us to such sights as the "Tres Ojos," the caverns right in the middle of town.

An army of "unofficial guides" patrolled the area, looking for tourists like me who would appreciate their help and demonstrate it with a few pesos. To be honest, I was the perfect client, but my companions felt obligated to "protect" me. My theory is that it's quicker, more pleasant and ultimately a better story if I just pay the money and enjoy the ride.

While we toured the underground marvel that is "Tres Ojos," our taxi driver got another call and figured he had enough time to respond. Unfortunately, all of our belongings, including our passports were in our bags, which were in the back of his van. By the way, there was also a large tank of propane in there too. A great percentage of cars in the Dominican Republic have been modified so that they don't have to depend on gasoline. My knowledge of chemistry is extremely limited but I have a feeling that riding on top of a propane tank is not the safest way to get around but who was I to question what didn't seem to concern anyone else.

My anxiety level didn't reach the panic stage because the taxi swerved into view and pulled up just as I began to rant about the passports in the trunk. The rest of our party had retreated to a spot just beyond earshot of my voice while Anna patiently reassured me all would turn out well.

Reunited with our belongings, we began the search for a famous restaurant called, "Los Hermanos Villar." Why we didn't just tell the driver the name of this place from the very beginning, I don't know. But instead, our hosts described the entire neighborhood, specifically the name of a nearby hotel, the Duque de Wellington, the distance from the caverns and other landmarks.

I was sitting in the front seat with the driver while these instructions were delivered from the back seats. The man behind the wheel was used to it. He obediently made every turn they suggested and waited for more when he was told, "Oh no. This isn't it."

When the name "Villar" finally got mentioned, he shrugged and said he needed no further direction. And in moments we were right in front of the place. My suspicious nature led me to conclude that he allowed our fare to fatten up quite a bit before tiring of the game and delivering us to our destination.

After consuming a meal that, in volume and variety, lived up to my anticipation of it, we began a long walk down the boulevard called simply, "El Conde," as in The Count. Any and every possible souvenir you could imagine was available and there did not seem to be a price tag on any of it. The age-old system of haggling survives in Santo Domingo. No bar codes or computers, just the simplest of all economic systems: "How much is it?" and "How much do you offer?"

The heat, even in early spring, was unbearable and when we finally reached the farther reaches of El Conde, our goal shifted to finding another taxi to take us back to the bus station. Even that price was open for negotiation and Priti showed the locals what she had learned over the past few years. Plying her craft, she got us a reasonable price and we arrived at the terminal just before the last bus of the day going north to Santiago was about to leave.

The sun was in full descent by that time and we made the trip in comfortable darkness. The only sound was the muffled roar of the engine that powered the bus and a conversation a young medical student was having with someone else.

His voice, pleasant and cheerful, was loud enough to reach my ears but the other person spoke softly. It was like listening to one side of a telephone conversation and today I would have assumed that's exactly what was going on. That particular annoyance wasn't part of the Dominican landscape nor was the practice of "playing with your phone," tapping and swiping to prevent colored balls from falling into a vat or whatever it is they're doing.

To the gentle sway of the bus and the rhythm of the young man's voice, as he took his listener from the days of his childhood to enrollment in the university, I began to think of a story I'd written years ago about the strangers on a train.

Teena Farmon was the warden at the women's prison in Chowchilla, not far from the town where we lived, and she was returning from Seattle to Fresno on the Coast Starlight, an express train that travels in luxury down the Pacific coast.

All this happened in November of 1996.

"You're on a train and I know people in that situation tend to get involved in a conversation," she recalled, "Still, when it happened to me, I was a little surprised. I tend to stay to myself and I certainly don't call attention to my job."

But there was this thin, bald man, maybe in his mid-60's, who was walking through her car and asked politely, "Are you traveling alone?"

"My first reaction was, as I say, surprise. First off, I'm black. And he was white. But when I looked into his face, all I could see was honest friendship. So I told him that I was alone."

He invited the lone traveler to have lunch with him … and his wife. "It was their second honeymoon trip," said Mrs. Farmon. "But you know that's nothing like the first honeymoon trip. They didn't keep to themselves at all. The man had befriended a whole group of people, maybe five all together, and we all had dinner together. Then there was a show the railroad put on and, after that, the group grew to eight."

"Every time someone came through the railroad car alone, this man would make it a point to make them feel welcome and include them in our conversation. I was kidding the wife about how her husband was able to find out so much about these total strangers. In fact, I let it slip that I was the warden of a woman's prison."

If she thought that subject would be off-limits, Mrs. Farmon was sadly mistaken. The thin bald man dropped that item first thing the next morning. "And then my job became the center of attention."

She took no offense and the party of eight, previously strangers, spent hours talking and laughing and telling stories about themselves and their loved ones as if they'd spent their entire lives together.

"Then the wife mentioned you," said Mrs. Farmon. "That you were the editor of the newspaper in Madera. So I called just to tell you this story. I thought it would cheer you up. I heard your Mom was sick."

I thanked her and gave her a brief and, to be honest, wildly optimistic prognosis. "She'll be all right. I'm sure of it."

"The Amtrak people told me they'd never seen anything like it and your parents were not just in the middle of it but the reason it happened at all."

There was a good reason I would be thinking of that train trip through Canada. I'd asked my mother to keep a journal of it and, true to her word, she had. I read it immediately upon their return to Madera and then, for several years after her death in 1997, I kept the cloth-covered book tucked away. Recently, it had migrated to a book case and finally my carry-on bag that I took to the Dominican Republic.

From having heard the word so many times, I came to understand that "Guandules," were not only the tiny beans so popular among Dominicans, but also the name of a place. Imagine my interest when I was invited to visit this labyrinth of narrow streets with buildings of every hue rising two and three stories high on both sides.  You could stretch out both arms and touch the concrete on either side. The pavement was a thin layer of cement poured over dirt, which made for quite a few impressive potholes.

I saw one car connected to another, but upon closer inspection, it turned out that one was trying to pull the other. And what they employed as a chain were the seat belts ripped from both vehicles.

If it weren't for the direction provided by Gladys, Missy and Priti, I would have never found my way out of this dizzying maze. I have a tendency to always go left, so I appreciated the helpful reminders, "Over here Brother Jim. Over here."

At one point, a woman emerged from a door at the top of a narrow spiral of wrought iron stairs and yelled, "What are you selling?"

"Not selling," one of the young men with us shouted back. And then he took one of the printed sheets we were distributing, wrapped it in a rock he picked up from the ground and gently tossed it up to her. The woman caught it, removed the stone and started reading the paper. As we walked on, we heard the sound of the stone plopping back to its original location.

Someone in our group pointed to a small house and said it belonged to one of the members of our group. I found a way to engage the slender woman of about 60 years of age in conversation as we finished up our canvassing.

"Oh yes," she told me. "I live here. In fact, I was one of the first to move here. At first, it was all metal shacks and cardboard huts and the streets were dirt and very dusty. That was about 30 years ago. This all just sprang up without anyone planning it."

"Then the city decided to stop trying to move us all out, since nobody would leave or, if they were forced out, they'd just come back later. So the city said they'd pave the streets and name them if we would all put numbers on our houses so they would know who lived where."

"They wanted us to name the streets by letters. But we named the streets for saints so that's why this is really supposed to be called Barrio Los Santos, but everyone thinks it's part of Guandalues, which goes from here all the way to the river."

"The shacks and huts were torn down and the city put up these concrete buildings and then spread the rest of the cement on the ground to make streets," she said. "It's much nicer now."

Up to that point, I couldn't imagine anything worse than this slum but, given what I'd been told, obviously improvements had been made.

"I know it must be confusing to you, since it's your first time here, but the city even has a map of this neighborhood. You can get it at City Hall."

She gave me a detailed explanation of the entire Guandules territory, naming every component and main thoroughfare, but it was all as confusing to me as the area itself.

"People who live here have jobs. I'm a seamstress. There are taxi drivers and cement workers, all kinds." I suspected that some of the women we'd seen were engaged in a profession often described as the oldest one in the world.

On our way back to where we started, the group took a different path, one that led us past the river where unspeakable damage was being done to the environment. A stinking slough dribbled through hills of refuse and, up on the bluffs of the river, people had reverted to wooden shacks and huts, but with gardens in gaps between them.

The vegetables that strained through the hard dirt were never eaten directly but were converted into seasoning, I was told. "There isn't enough boiling water in the entire world to get me to put any of that in any dish I'd eat," was my reply, which was not considered an insult by my listeners.

In the relative comfort of the adjacent neighborhood, we stopped at a couple of houses for what we call "return visits." A young girl stood in the doorway and listened attentively to Priti. Meanwhile, a naked boy about three years old chewed on his fist. When we left, Belle said, "The boy and his older brother, about five years old, have what they call 'hongos' or a fungus on their heads."

At another stop, a 17-year old boy invited us into their family's home, which was a concrete wall with aluminum sheets fashioned in such a way as to provide a roof and an opposing wall. The rest of the family stayed out of sight as we sat in chairs that must have once been in a city bus and discussed a Bible hope for the future.

It occurred to me later, as I drank a glass of lemonade on the veranda that our message must resound strongly among some of the people we'd met that day. Think about it. From just what I'd seen, heard and read, the young man living next to a concrete wall had little reason to aspire to any sort of comfort, let alone success, in his world. The only way out of this life of unending and bitter poverty was crime, sports or God. The first was too dangerous, the second too unlikely.

That evening, as we watched the late news of television, I suddenly sat up and pointed at the screen. "That's where we were this morning. That's the same neighborhood where we…"

But Missy took a closer look and shook her head. "No, I don't think so. It's the same kind of place but not the exact same one."

Priti gave me a second opinion. "She's right. There are a lot of 'Guandules' everywhere on this island."

As we sat around the table on the veranda, watching the darkness envelope El Ensueno, Kookie said, "Part of my job at the county was arranging for pauper burials. Not anymore, but when I first started. I'll never forget this boy named Gabriel."

"What made this burial different from the others was that a funeral home made their chapel available for a little ceremony and I attended it. The first and last time that ever happened."

The child was born with meningitis and had to be fed and clothed and bathed by others for the four years of his life. In every way, he remained an infant, not like his energetic brothers who explored every corner of the room except the pale blue coffin in the very front.

The doctors had predicted from the very beginning that Gabriel's life would be short. They were right. There was a lot of talk about "quality of life" because it was painfully obvious that the tiny boy could not communicate at all, but who was to say that he did not feel the love his family expressed to him.

"He wasn't a burden at all," Kookie told us. "There was an older daughter, about 11 years old, and she took on most of the responsibility of caring for Gabriel without a word of complaint. That night at the funeral, she seemed to me a lot older than 11."

"Another time, I was sent out to a farm where a two-month-old boy was going to die from a genetic disorder and the family needed some papers from the county because they planned to follow the harvest. In case the boy died on the way, they wanted some proof of his condition."

"I'll never forget how his older brothers brought him out of their little house. They laid him on the lawn, out in the sun, so he could get some fresh air, maybe get warm. There was a little girl pretending to be a fountain. She'd drink water from a hose, then pucker up her cheeks and squirt it into the air. The boys kept telling her to aim away from the baby. They made it to the next farm and that's where the baby died."

D own on the first floor, a man named Sergio lived with his wife Iris. He also worked out of his home, although it was unclear to me, at first, just what position he held. We had bumped into one another on the day I tried to buy a newspaper from the vendor selling the traditional tripe stew, mondongo.

Although he appeared to be my age, Sergio was actually about ten years older. He laughed when I admitted I thought the man was selling the newspaper, El Mundo, "The World."

"There's no such paper here," he chuckled.

One morning, he stepped back from the driver's side of his car and yelled up at me. "Hey! Want to come along with me? I'm going on some business calls."

Since I had nothing urgent to do, I took him up on his offer and soon the two of us were careening through the streets of Santiago.

We went over a bridge and around a bend, then down a hill and up another one. In other words, I didn't know where we were.

Finally, we pulled up in front of a house and he motioned me to follow him to the door. From the conversation and shuffling of papers, I figured out that Sergio sells insurance.

We made a few more stops, one of which proved instructive. A large woman in a small office handed him a stack of files while a girl who appeared to be her daughter labored over a copy machine, churning out page after page. This, I surmised, was a branch office of the Sergio financial empire.

As we drove to several of these locations before ending up in a bank where a deposit was made, Sergio and I talked as if we'd known each other for years.

"When do you plan on retiring?" I asked since that was an option I'd recently taken.

"Retiring?" he hooted. "There's no retirement here. You just stop working when you can't work anymore and hope you earned enough to get by. Retiring!"

When we pulled into a hospital parking lot, I wondered if Sergio carried a kind of medical insurance and had to check on patients.

"No, it's my granddaughter. She has some kind of fever. Maybe dengue."

The facility had an odd security system. As long as one could provide some form of identification, then the guard waved you through a door to the elevators and, from there, up to the patient's room. It didn't seem to matter if you might be carrying a weapon somewhere on your person just as long as you could show an official looking card with your picture and name on it.

Sergio had just the document the guard wanted but when it came my turn, I shrugged and said, "I'll just wait here."

"Oh no," said Sergio and, directing himself to the young female in uniform, said, "He's with me."

And that was enough for her.

The 12-year-old girl was pale, but smiling when she saw her grandfather. On the other side of the bed was her grandmother, Iris, and her mother. I felt completely out of place until Sergio introduced me as "Brother Jim."

So that's why he felt comfortable inviting me along.

The scene at the hospital is replayed day after day all over the world, the attempt at humor, the nervous chatter, the overwhelming relief when we are told that the patient is improving and responding well to treatment.

Not long thereafter, Sergio, his wife Iris, Anna and I were sitting at the table of a restaurant. The four of us were the only customers because we'd arrived at the midpoint between lunch and dinner.

Our orders were taken by an older man who rushed off after having seated us at a solid wooden table with four gigantic rocking chairs set around it. We enjoyed the cool breeze and the taste of Presidente beer while our pork and chicken dishes were being whipped up in the kitchen.

It's an open-air type restaurant so the only thing that separated us from the sidewalk was the ever present array of wrought iron bars. Then a young man, skinny and bewhiskered, stuck his face between the bars and lifted up a shoe shine box.

Sergio turned to the elderly waiter who approached the young man and said, "Go away my little son." And it appeared he'd heeded the warning but, when the fried yucca and plantains were brought to the table, the pathetic face reappeared.

He mumbled something, perhaps an offer to shine some shoes, but we avoided his gaze and concentrated on our appetizers.

Eventually, he shuffled off.

"Some people like to stop and talk," I said to Sergio in English, "but the walking man walks. James Taylor."

My new friend did not respond.

"What's sad," his wife Iris said softly, "is that we have so much freedom now in one way and we are so enslaved in another way."

"When I was a little girl in the time of the dictator Trujillo, you would not see that, what you just saw. People were afraid. You could take a million pesos, put it in a bag and leave it at the park. No one would touch it. They were afraid it was a trick."

"Every door had a sign on it. 'In this house, Trujillo rules,' is what it said. My father made dentures.

He was a true artist and a medical man at the same time. Whenever he saw that sign on our door, he'd take it down. My mother would put it back up. Then, he'd take it down."

Iris was a thin woman, stately is how I'd describe her. Quiet, well-mannered, very European in appearance and, to me, shy and I held back expressing my observation that her father might have removed the sign but he never threw it away.

"Trujillo's men, the secret police, drove around in those little German cars that make a sound like a whisper. If you heard that whisper late at night on your street, you had reason to worry. You or one of your neighbors was going to disappear."

Sergio nodded. "People were shot and killed on the street and left there as if nothing had happened."

We tore into our barbecued chicken and pork chops and talked about baseball a little. Spring training would be underway back in the United States but in the Dominican Republic, it was time for their championship series, then the Caribbean World Series and maybe the World Baseball Classic.

"By the way," Sergio said as we finished up our meal with dessert, "tomorrow, there's going to be a strike. Better stay home. I'm not saying it'll be dangerous or anything, but why take a chance."

"**S**omber," is how I would describe the next day's dawn. Cloudy and still, everything a little wet from rain the night before... and silent.

No roar of distant trucks, no buzz of motorcycles, no basso 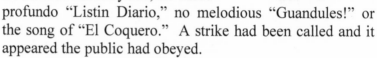 profundo "Listin Diario," no melodious "Guandules!" or the song of "El Coquero." A strike had been called and it appeared the public had obeyed.

Sergio came up the stairs with some rolls and we broke our fast together. Between sips of coffee and mouthfuls of bread, he explained what was going on... or not in this case.

"The problem is that gasoline prices have gone up so high. It costs twice as much to put gas in your car as it does to get the same amount of propane. It costs so much to install the tank and convert to propane that the taxi drivers are hoping that the government will help them switch to propane, give them a subsidy or something."

But what would the average guy do? People like Sergio?

"Oh, we'd keep buying gas, of course. But so many people here depend on taxis and conchos and the private buses that this is a big issue."

"So the government will pay to convert to propane?"

"Not a chance," laughed Sergio. "And the strike will just be a day. They can't be on strike the last day of this month. It's our Independence Day."

"The monument," and he pointed in that direction, "will be flooded with traffic. People will go there for the celebration and most of them don't have cars so don't worry about the strike. Tomorrow I mean. Not today. Stay around here today."

"I was thinking of getting a haircut," I said.

And I filled him on an odd series of events the other day when I wandered around the corner to a barber shop. "Three men were sitting in the chairs but they weren't customers, but barbers, I suppose. Anyway, as I sat there waiting, the man who appeared to be the owner took a cell phone call and then walked out to the street. A few minutes later, another man showed up and they talked for a few moments. Then the barber came back in the shop, went straight to the bathroom and then came out, sat down in his chair and sort of stared off into space. The other two barbers looked at me and one of them shrugged."

"So you left?"

"Yes, because I figured I wasn't going to get a haircut that day. Maybe tomorrow? At a different shop?"

Sergio laughed. "Where? Hey, get some scissors. I'll cut your hair. Wait, I don't need to. It's gone already."

Besides the eerie silence, the only evidence of a strike was the television news, which consisted, once again, of one man, sitting behind a small desk, talking non-stop. On one program, there were two men, sitting in a couple of wingback chairs, talking and, if I understood them correctly, refuting everything being said on the other channel.

By noon, I'd become a little bored with the whole thing and that's part of the reason I welcomed the unexpected visit of young Pedro Martinez.

The youngster spoke a bewildering mixture of English and Spanish, but no matter, at least he was talking. He reported in detail the ongoing nine-game championship series between Licey and Los Escogidos, both of whom play their home games in the same stadium in Santo Domingo.

Licey jumped out to a lead, three games to one, but then their opponents, whose name might be translated All Stars, made a comeback and won the next two games. With both teams now even and only three games remaining, Pedro anticipated the pitching matchups, reviewed the injury situation for both teams and commented on the momentum theory.

"So who are you rooting for?" I asked.

"I can't be for Licey," he replied. "If you're from Santiago, you can't. But I do like some of their players this year. But Licey was Trujillo's team."

"Escogidos then."

"They won't win," he shrugged, "but yes, Escogidos."

I inquired about the local team, The Aguilas, or Eagles, and he shook his head sadly. "They fell out of contention a month before the season ended. Just played out the string."

"That's an interesting expression," I commented.

W e awoke the next morning to the sound of a steady drip coming from the laundry room. The reason was obvious. Both the hot and cold water faucets were  leaking and Anna set out to remedy the situation.

From the outset of our marriage, she has been the handyman in the family. I remember the day (and it was long ago) that she asked me to nail a little brass item onto a door. It's that piece that covers the latch, the part that goes in and out so the door will close. After I got done, she came over and inspected all the hammer marks, the round impressions I'd left and said, "You weren't lying. You really don't know how to do anything."

Maybe I should have taken offense but it was obvious "anything" in this context meant activities related to hammers, nails, screwdrivers, screws and all that sort of stuff.

But back to the leaky faucet, which Anna quickly diagnosed, determined which parts we needed and where to find them. However, when it came to actually taking off the old ones and replacing them, we found out that neither of us, separately or together, had the strength to do so. Enter Sergio with a wrench.

"First thing we have to do," he instructed us, "is open all the faucets upstairs and downstairs. The water coming through the pipes is from the tinaco on top of the roof so there's no valve to turn that off. We just have to lower the pressure by spreading the water around. Then, we take off a faucet, replace it, and do the same with the second one. Simple, right?"

Not that simple. Even with water coming out of every possible faucet in the building, the spigots in question simply wouldn't budge. Meantime, the dripping had increased to leaking and then flowing.

Sergio rushed downstairs and returned with a bigger wrench. With a flourish, he attacked the coupler in question and then, with a few twists, removed the old spigots. With all the faucets running mind you, he screwed on the new ones and called out for us to "close the valves!"

Stepping back from the sink like a surgeon who had just replaced a heart, a lung and a kidney, Sergio pronounced our problem solved.

Not all of them, I thought to myself.

We were preparing to celebrate that evening. Days before, the ladies had decided we should invite people up to the terrace for dinner, dancing and other social activities.

As the preparations for the party began in earnest, it became apparent that some supplies were lacking so Anna and I hopped into Missy's car and all three of us headed downtown. When we had the plumbing supplies and other purchases in hand, we hauled them out of the store and out into the street.

To our surprise, Missy's car was gone and so were all the other vehicles that had been parked in that block.

A shopkeeper came out and informed us that tow trucks, dispatched from the police station located in the historic La Fortaleza, had removed them all. I protested, pointing out that there were no signs. "There have to be clearly marked 'No Parking' signs, one on each block," I insisted.

The lady from the store laughed. "Signs? They don't need signs! Every once in a while, this is what happens."

We asked to use her telephone and it wasn't long before Sergio came to our rescue. He knew exactly where to look for the vehicle, who to talk to (and there were several conversations), when to speak up and when to keep quiet.

Finally, we were taken to a ravine where, I swear, dozens of cars and hundreds of motorcycles were lined up. The tow truck drivers lounged in lawn chairs and chatted as the owners trooped in and claimed their property.

Sergio pointed in the general direction of two women and a man (me) and said, "They're from the U.S. and didn't know about the no parking zone. Can they pay their fine here?"

It seemed odd to me, but the answer was, "No. You must take this paper and go to the National Bank. There, you must purchase a cashier's check and then bring that back here."

The man in a brown uniform implied that our car would be returned to us, but I noticed there was no guarantee.

At the bank, we lined up with others in the same situation. When Missy tried to get the necessary cashier's check, she was told the bank's computers were not working at that moment. Yet, I could clearly see a screen alive with words and figures, obviously functioning.

Sergio saw it too and soon had a badge in his hand and was about to display it as if to say, "I really don't want to throw my weight around, but I will if it's necessary."

Finally, the cash, all $37 of it, was exchanged for the check and we were back at La Fortaleza. But now there was a new obstacle.

"Just get the registration out of your car and bring it to me," a woman behind a card table right out there among the cars said. "And we can let you be on your way."

Missy nodded and set off, slowly, toward her car. The problem, I found out later, was that the registration was in Priti's name, her real one. Would that mean we wouldn't be able to take possession?

Apparently, Sergio already knew of this problem and he began a lawyerly discourse with the young woman at the card table which ended with our being allowed to follow Missy to her car and drive away.

When we were safely out of earshot, Sergio told me that, coincidentally, all the tow trucks were owned by the son of the police commander who commandeered all those vehicles. He shrugged, "That's the way it is."

It was on our way home, when we thought nothing else could go wrong, that the street lights all went dark. "A blackout," said Missy. "Happens once in a while. Nothing to worry about."

But, of course, I did, especially when it lasted a half an hour, followed by about 15 minutes of electrical current and then another half hour without power.

My concerns were allayed, however, when, with a whirring sound, all the appliances in the apartment suddenly came to life again.

Outside, we saw the clouds, low and threatening, but had faith that the rain, if it ever came, would wait until after the party. In fact, in an act of pure faith, we carried all the furniture out to the terrace. Our faith was rewarded. Hours after the last of our new friends left, heavy drops began to fall, landing only on the red tiles, not on the wicker chair, futon or kitchen table.

It took me several attempts to get these few pieces in exactly the right spots and the frantic process reminded me of the tiny office four (sometimes five) interpreters occupied at Madera Superior Court. As I counted down to my eventual retirement, the more I shoved desks and chairs into different configurations until finally my colleagues and supervisor couldn't take it anymore. We got a memorandum prohibited adding, subtracting or rearranging the furniture in the office. It was addressed to everyone but directed squarely at me.

"Thank God someone stopped me," I laughed when it was read out loud.

The group started to arrive and the music tinkled, then swayed and then soared as the guests worked through the chips, dips and finger foods. The actual dinner would have to wait. First, they wanted to dance.

When the music finally slowed down, Sergio took the floor and, serving as a de-facto master of ceremonies, thanked everyone for coming to "greet some of our visitors" and to "send off others with this farewell." I wasn't fully aware of it at that moment, but he was not only referring to some of those who had traveled down to the Caribbean to enjoy Dominican hospitality, but also the fact that several of those present would be moving out to "the campo," that rural area assigned to the congregation.

He surprised Anna and I with an anniversary cake with the number 40 elaborately drawn in icing on top and I thanked him and all the others who'd made the evening possible.

And then the music picked up again because, as John Mellencamp once said, "Dancing was everything," and it was only after the older ones retreated from the dance floor that the meal itself was carted out of the kitchen and out onto the terrace.

They played a game in which a broom is passed around the dance floor and whoever is left holding it when the music stops is "out." At the same time, everyone was switching partners, leading to a collision and a few of the contestants went sprawling to the floor. No one was hurt, of course, and, in fact, they all seemed to enjoy it.

A karaoke sing-along came at the end of the evening and several of the attendees choked a bit, some out of emotion and others, I suspect, from trying to keep from laughing at some of the more ambitious singers' trying to hit the high notes.

Anna and I waited until almost the very end to dance together. We weren't exactly graceful since my style has always been a form of stomping around in rhythm, not always the one set by the music, while Anna is limited by the pain in her back. Although, perhaps because of the summer-like weather or just the excitement of being on vacation, she had been relatively comfortable during our time there.

Just when we thought the evening was drawing to a close, the guests drew up their chairs, forming a semi-circle and several of the people I hadn't recognized up to that point, were called upon to speak.

It turned out that a couple who had spent quite a few years teaching the Bible to people in the Dominican Republic were about to head back to their home state of Maryland. Earlier in their lives, the couple had been missionaries in the country of Surinam, that finger of land right at the top of South America and they told us a story about those days.

The chief of one of the villages where they'd been preaching was being pressured by the witch doctor to banish a young man because he'd responded to our message and had joined them in their work.

"Things didn't look good for our young friend until it was revealed that his umbilical cord had been buried in a field near the village. It turned out that this was an ancient practice, a guarantee that anyone born in that village could never be forced to leave. So the chief ruled in his favor and now, in that area, there are several congregations."

In the increasingly dim light, I really couldn't make out the faces of some of the guests, but, at one point, I came upon a woman who looked just like my mother did when she was about 50 years old. It was both wonderful and disturbing. Later that night, in the living room, I opened a red cloth-colored journal and began reading:

9

To Canada and Back

By Margaret Watrous

Saturday, November 30, 1996 ... 10:05 p.m.

Amtrak was late getting into Madera by 15 minutes. The train was crowded with very few vacant seats so we ended up sitting with another couple. He's a computer programmer and she's a consultant and was reading a book about evolution. Across from the aisle, there two men playing dominos and Bill, of course the eternal host, conducted interviews with each of them.

When we got to Martinez, where the Coast Starlight was supposed to be waiting for us, we found out it would be two hours late, which meant midnight. Another group joined up with us and, all told, there were 23 people sharing the same fate.

Sunday, December 1, 1996... Klamath Falls, Ore.

We had breakfast with JoAnn and Linda from Kentucky. I called them Thelma and Louise when they weren't around. JoAnn reminded me of a friend of ours from Connecticut. She was a large, rugged, mountain-loving, hunting, fishing type and a cat lover. Linda was quiet, a perfect companion for JoAnn, sort of a straight man for her stories.

The food isn't very good but it's included in the fare, so I guess we'll be satisfied. Bill and I had our first in-train "discussion." All I said was, "Are you through making a fool of yourself?"

The scenery is beautiful. Snow on the ground. Little kids are running around without their coats on in spite of the cold.

Tuesday, December 3, 1996, ... Jasper, Canada

We spent yesterday in Vancouver. We had arrived around 2:30 a.m and then got up around 9 a.m. Rain, slush, sleet and snow... just what I came to see. We walked through a mall across from the Hotel Georgia, where we stayed, and made it in plenty of time for when the train pulled out of the station at 7 p.m.

There was no radio or television, just the two of us and the scenery flying by the window. We sat on the bed and talked for hours and then we'd look at the mountains and trees.

We were on our way to Jasper and we saw Mount Robeson which, I'm told, can only be seen 12 days out of the year. One big cake of snow and ice. Actually, I'm not sure if we saw this before we got to Jasper or after or if I got the name right.

Wednesday., December 4, 1996

We had dinner with a couple, Claude and Nicole, both native Canadians, and it was really nice. By the way, we don't get dressed up for meals. Everyone is presentable but not over-done.

Bill got to go up to the locomotive engine housing last night. Claude arranged it.

The snow is deep and is in drifts, which is how I prefer it. Mountains are mountains, but I still like level land better. It seemed to me that every lake was frozen. I saw lots of trees, a moose and a family of deer yesterday afternoon.

Another treat today was my shower. I had to go down the hall because, although each compartment has a toilet, you have to make the trip to get to a shower. Well worth it, though.

Thursday, December 5, 1996

I packed and re-packed as we made our way toward Toronto tonight at 9. We had dinner again last night with Claude and Nicole and, right after that, we saw derailed cars alongside the tracks. Twenty-three cars went off the tracks about a week ago on the same route we're on, but it was a freight train, which made me feel a little better.

Friday, December 6, 1996...Toronto

I was standing in the reception hall of the Royal York Hotel where we will be staying in Toronto waiting for Bill when an old man walked by and said, "Hi Honey!" and patted my fanny.

I turned to find Bill and I said, "Did you see that?"

"See what?"

"That old man patted my fanny." I pointed at the man headed for the escalator who suddenly turned around and came back our way.

"He's coming back again."

When he got within a few inches from me, he took off his hat and it turned out to be my brother-in-law Bob McLaughlin. And there was Selma, his wife, Bill's sister, standing there too. What a surprise! We stayed up until 2 a.m. or so talking. Seems Bill had made the arrangements to surprise me and he did!

And the hotel is absolutely beautiful. Chrystal chandeliers, mohair furniture, antiques in the lobby, real luxury.

We had lunch with Claude and Nicole and parted company. Very sincere people. Then Selma and I went shopping. That night, we saw "Phantom of the Opera" which was stunning

Sunday, December 8, 1996...Niagara Falls

Snow fell heavily all day during our bus tour all day from Toronto all the way to Niagara Falls, which was covered in snow and ice. It was a beautiful sight but we weren't allowed to get closer to the falls than the IMAX theater where we saw a movie about the area. The entire experience was awesome, a great production.

Monday, December 9, 1996... Toronto

We toured Sky Dome, which is an engineering marvel, and we saw everything from top to bottom.

Tuesday, December 10, 1996

Bob and Selma left at 4:30 a.m. and we got up early to see them off. Hours later, we got back on the train and began our return trip from Toronto to Vancouver and, from there, down the coast back to Fresno.

I know I shouldn't complain but our compartment on the return trip will be smaller and the shower is even farther down the hall. I guess I'm getting spoiled.

Wednesday, December 11, 1996

Early in the morning, I went to the Observation Car and, from up there, I could see the whole train in front of me and the headlight searching and guiding the train through a tunnel bordered by rocks and trees. As it bended and twisted, the train was illuminated by red and green lights alongside the tracks. The reflection of these Christmas lights seemed to tell the big light in front where to go and it obeyed the commands. Soon the sky took on a rosy glow in the east and the sun rose, putting everything into a yellow cast, which started at the very top of the trees and gradually descended down to the snow. It was like an egg cracked and the yolk was poured out.

I guess God was saying, "Good morning."

In the growing light, I could see tall trees covered in ice that looked like lace curtains hanging down from poles, sparkling against a blue sky, snapping and catching the sun.

Going from car to car, I was greeted by the cold and snow that had sneaked through the cracks and crevices and my breath released in small explosions. I had to grab the side rails and hang on because the metal plates were slippery. Kids would have loved it. I know I did.

The sun was in full bloom and the train whipped up the snow as it plowed through the mountains, creating a still life portrait with all the elements, the snow, the sun and the wind.

Every once in a while, there is a clearing, a snowy meadow, which looks so inviting, but, if I stepped out there somehow, I would have been knee-deep in the white stuff.

I've gone by so many posts, that I've figured out that a W with a circle around it means "no whistle," but one without the circle tells the crew to go ahead and let the whistle blow. Two red lights tell the engineer to stop the train.

Small streams broke through the snow... always a surprise... and reminds me that water insists on rising, whether the surface be rock or meadow and then the liquid, as clear as glass, winds down the mountain. From time to time, I realize that what appears to be flatland is actually a frozen lake.

The taller trees are loaded with what looks like cotton candy and the smaller ones could be snowmen with green arms and legs poking out from white bodies.

The snow on the ground sparkled like champagne and the wind stirred up enough of it to remind me of confetti.

Bill and I had dinner together and went back to our compartment. We sat on the lower berth for quite a while, watching the night and the lights from the homes in towns along the tracks. It was so peaceful to lean on his shoulder and to be far away from the real world for a while.

Thursday, December 12 to Friday, December 13, 1996

I met a fisherman from Newfoundland who has been at sea since he was 13 years of age and would be there yet if it weren't for illness. A surgeon had to remove half his stomach to save his life. I also saw a gray-haired man. And what hair! It was so wild that I would swear he hadn't combed it since he was ten. His clothes were dirty and smelled.

Our train was met by a freight going in the opposite direction and we slowed down. When we got to Sioux Lookout, the train stopped and we did exactly that... looked out. Bill slipped and fell, said his knee was hurting.

When we got going again, I noticed roads that cut through the snow but didn't seem to be pathways to anywhere at all, just random veins in the landscape.

When we got to Winnipeg, I wanted to step down to the platform when I was stopped by our porter, Wolfgang, who asked me, "Where are you going? You may not leave the train for 15 more minutes. Go back to your compartment please." With that German accent of his, I thought it was hilarious. And I thought I heard him say, "We have ways of making you obey."

Later that day, I met the fisherman's wife, Bertha, and she was one lonely woman. They had nine children, six boys and three girls, and they've all grown up and moved away because the canneries closed and there's no work in Newfoundland for them. They were on their way to visit one of their granddaughters who had just moved away too.

When we got off the train at Winnipeg, Bill and I went to a shop and bought Bertha a key chain, since she couldn't get off the train without great difficulty. I also bought a bouquet of carnations for a woman, only about 40 years old, in the compartment down from ours. She has multiple sclerosis and is bed-ridden.

In Edmonton, the woman with MS and her mother got off the train. Such a young woman to have been stricken with this disease. She was fine up until three years ago.

When the train moved on, going west, I saw people ice fishing. It was quite a circus, people camping on the banks and others out there in those little huts on the ice.

Meanwhile, Bill went down to the kitchen to take photographs and interview people. Columbo at work.

By 2 a.m., we were in the Canadian Rockies and the snow looks like frosting dribbling down the sides of enormous bundt cakes of ice and snow. Some of the mountains are flat on top and the trees growing on top make them look like fat men with crew haircuts.

By the next afternoon, we had passed Jasper where Bill convinced a Mounty to stand still for a photo. We were so high up the trees down below looked like toys. Nothing kept us from falling down those canyons except the fact that the train clings to the tracks. I wondered what would happen if we toppled over. How would we survive?

Saturday, December 14, 1996

We arrived in Vancouver after having dinner the night before with newlyweds, which was nice. The weather on Saturday morning was miserable, rainy and cold, but we were warm in our hotel room before heading off to find more souvenirs.

In the afternoon, we took a tour and the bus was empty except for us, which made it a personal guided tour for four hours. We had dinner at a noisy place called, "The Keg," and then went back to our room to pack for the trip south the next day.

The next day, we were back on the Coast Starlight and met a woman who said she was the warden at the prison in Chowchilla. Very nice person and you can tell she knows how to manage people without being overbearing.

Bill was like a cruise director at work and pretty soon, our group was pretty large. He took charge of half of them, the more raucous ones, and I sat with the quieter ones.

By the way, early this morning at the hotel, I woke up to people shouting back and forth, saying things like, "I gotta go!" and "What for?" Later on, when Bill went to get a luggage cart, I heard him talk to someone and then got uncharacteristically serious. "No! The lobby is downstairs," he said.

When he got back to the room, he said, "Did you hear that? I think she was a prostitute."

So that's what all the yelling was about.

That evening, we had a big party. Even the waiters joined in and it was one of the best memories I'll carry with me when the train reaches Martinez, where we switch to the San Joaquin and return home.

Maybe this happens all the time, but still it made me feel special when the waiters hugged us as we got off the train at Martinez late that night.

We didn't reach home until Sunday, Dec. 15, but we were still three hours early because the previous train had been delayed and our wait there was only 15 minutes. When we reached Madera, Bill and I played this comedy routine trying to get off the train. I'd run one way and he'd run the other because the doors wouldn't open and we had five pieces of luggage. Then we heard our names being announced over the loudspeakers because our kids were on the platform waiting for us to appear, but couldn't because we were trying to find a door that would open.

Finally, Bill screamed, "We're trying, but we can't get out," and then the doors closest to our seats parted and we escaped. What a way to finish a trip.

Monday, December 16, 1996

The luggage is still packed but I'm not ready to get to it yet because I feel the swaying of the train... a sort of land jet lag. But I'm also reviewing our trip and I have to say that it was well worth it.

Although the train ride was great, the scenery out of this world and the people we met were unforgettable, I have already picked out my favorite memory. It's that night we sat on the lower berth, staring at the snow and stars and I rested my head on your shoulder, Bill, and felt we were young again. This, I will remember.

10

Heading Home

Danny arrived and I met him at the bottom of the stairs. Anna accompanied me down to the street, reminding me that I would have to go through customs at LaGuardia Airport in New York.

"Don't forget to put your battery back in the cell phone," she added. Oh yes. I would be like an astronaut coming from the dark side of the moon back into range.

At the Cibao International Airport, things went smoothly and, to be honest, a bit too fast. Danny put me in the right line, stepped back, waved me over to another line, then, after making sure I'd been ushered into the departure wing of the terminal, retreated to his car.

The heartfelt thanks I had in my wallet stayed there. No doubt "Sister Anna" had taken care of that ahead of time.

We descended through the clouds to find LaGuardia Airport glistening after a thorough soaking the day before. Not that I had much of a chance to admire it. I joined in the clapping for the landing and then hustled through the process of being reintegrated into the U.S.A.

The man who examined my passport asked me a routine question, "What was the reason for your stay in Dominican Republic?"

Befuddled, I stammered, "My wife and I celebrated our 40ᵗʰ anniversary."

He peered over my shoulder. "Where is she now?"

"Still there," I said quickly. "Uh, she decided... well, she arrived before I did and had to have a roundtrip ticket so she can't leave for a couple of more days. I'm flying on miles and they have me going from here to Seattle, spending the night there and then on to Fresno and then..."

The man closed the passport wearily and handed it back to me. "Congratulations," he sighed.

I realized, as I walked down the aisle to my seat on the plane headed for Seattle, I would be in the very last row and on the aisle. So I would be privy to all the bathroom activity on the flight.

A young woman, a student bent over a book on the subject of North American Art and Artists, was to my left and, next to her, a man, somewhere between her age and mine, was attaching something to the window.

"I'm recording our flight for my wife," he explained when he saw the look on my face. The student ignored him. I decided that was the wisest course.

Three times during the program, the man at the window seat ordered what he called, "Jack and water," which turned out to be Johnny Walker Red with a plastic glass of water. The effect of this refreshment made him all the more sociable and I could hear him telling the art student about his house on top of a mountain east of Tacoma, Washington. Details of his home life poured out of him as whisky was poured into him.

The girl leaned over in my direction and said, "I'm going to the bathroom. When I come back, could you please switch seats with me?"

"Sure," I said. "Why not?"

I thought we were well on our way to the Rocky Mountains, but the pilot corrected me. Up to that point, he had been content to merely fly the plane and keep his thoughts to himself, but, for some reason, he now felt it necessary to provide commentary.

"That's Lake Michigan just off the right side," he announced at one point, followed a while later by updates about corn and Iowa and finally, the "Big Muddy."

Soon we were over "The Dakotas," and then there would be Montana, so much Montana. The young art student looked up from her book and nodding toward the window, said, "Looks like he finally passed out."

Three Jacks pressed his head against the porthole. He breathed deeply and his camera, I guess, continued to record the emptiness of the prairie.

Upon my arrival in Seattle, I realized that my clothes did not match the weather, as the song said, and I got to my hotel room as quickly as possible. A few hours sleep and I would be ready for the final leg of my journey.

The next morning, I presented myself at a small café in the hotel lobby for breakfast. "Ginger Palace" welcomed me with a big cup of coffee and a table with a window view of the cemetery across the street.

A young, very pleasant Asian woman told me I was the first customer that day and answered a couple of questions I had about the aquarium right next to the cash register. It was the fish that stirred my curiosity.

"Yes it is big and it is only a baby," she said in a charming accent. "We had another fish in there with it, but he wanted to be alone."

She made a face, the kind of expression we all make when we don't want to describe carnage of some kind.

The waitress took my order and then activated the music which, I supposed, would play all day. Elvis crooned about not being able to help falling in love and I set my sights on the graves that dotted the hill across the street. The grass was so green, so perfectly trimmed and, up at the very crest was a shed where, I imagined, they kept all their gardening tools, including the lawnmower. It seemed that every headstone had an arrangement of flowers neatly clustered around it and I wondered if the families were responsible or if it was part of the cemetery's service to them.

Dean Martin's "Memories Are Made of This" couldn't have come at a better time and the refill added to my contentment. The waitress slid a plate in front of me and said, "It's an Arawana from the Amazon," and I knew she meant the fish, not the pancakes.

I was a witness to a comedy, which could have been a tragedy for the protagonist. It seems the woman in front of me at the counter had packed her suitcase to overflowing. The bulging piece of luggage weighed about 20 lbs. more than the airline was willing to carry.

"Could I just pay?" she asked. No, she couldn't, the polite lady responded.

So the passenger hauled the bag off the scales, splayed it out and began removing items. It reminded me of Mary Poppins, the part where she takes a standing lamp out of her bag. At the same time, the woman, whom I would judge to be in her 40's, flipped out her cell phone and made a call.

The girl who received that call soon came trotting up to her side with an empty suitcase and started stuffing it with everything her mother (I assume) had decided to leave behind in Seattle.

"I knew this would happen," the daughter hissed without breaking her rhythm.

"It's just a good thing you hadn't left yet."

"Well, I'm parked out at the curb so hurry up or else I'm going to get a ticket."

The process of transferring items from one bag to another was just about done when two uniformed officers walked briskly to the ticket counter. "Are you the..."

"Yes I am," the girl answered without waiting for the end of the question. "I'll be right there."

"Your car is being towed right now," the taller of the two men said. "The dog is there now."

No one had to say what the dog was doing. We do live in dangerous times, don't we?

The girl turned to her mother and threw up her hands, "Well Mom, have a nice trip. Don't worry about me. I'll bail out on my own."

The older woman half-smiled and then bent down, zipped up her suitcase and set it up on the scales. "Am I under 50 lbs. now?"

The policemen gawked at her. "Just right," the lady behind the counter said.

Mom held out her arms and the daughter did the same. They hugged and then rushed off in two directions, one to the curb and the other to a gate.

Even if I had some comment on that scene, I wasn't going to make it at that moment.

Where people gathered for the flight to Fresno, I sat next to a window, through which I could see three airplanes, each marked with distinctive symbols.

"Look," the young man across from me told his wife, "there's the Oregon Ducks, the Idaho Vandals and Boise State Broncos. All three right there." And he took his cell phone and pointed it in that direction. "What's the chances you'd ever see that?"

His wife said she couldn't even guess. It took me a moment to realize that the woman was tiny in comparison to her husband. In fact, she appeared to be what I'm told is "a little person."

She was talking to a fellow passenger about a recent wedding in which a bridesmaid's dress, was accidentally carried off by the wrong person. "This man thought it was his garment bag and, before anyone could stop him, he was gone. The bridesmaid ran to the luggage counter as fast as she could but all they could do was send a car out to the guy's address and hope they could get the dress back in time for the wedding."

"And did they?" We all wanted to know.

"I think so," she said.

These nice people required a little more entertainment so I told them about Kookie and her sister's wedding, actually the night before.

"The three grown children were all getting ready for the wedding. The boy, now a man of course, said that, since he had worked in a dry cleaners before, he could iron the veil. Before his sisters caught on to what he had said, the guy had put the iron close enough to the lace that it disintegrated right before his eyes."

"The bride shrugged it off. Said they could cut it a little. As they're trimming the veil, he turns to Kookie and says, 'Hey! Look at us! We're working on a project together.'"

I laughed hard at my own story and they joined in and were rewarded by my not following that up with another tale from my own wedding.

Airborne over Washington and Oregon later on, the propeller-driven plane flew low enough so that we were afforded spectacular views of the mountains and, sitting in the aisle seat, front row, I took them all in.

To my right, a woman just a couple of years younger than me made the ride even that more enjoyable by pointing out some of the landmarks. "Crater Lake," she said and pointed.

The woman had been a teacher for all her adult life and her classroom assignments had included almost every level, from elementary to high school. "I'm going to Fresno for a funeral," she said without inviting any further inquiry. I got the impression a relative on her husband's side had passed away and that he was already there, making arrangements.

"I'm thinking of retirement," she said at one point. "Maybe I shouldn't say this, but there's one kid, just one, who has me thinking it's time for me to go. It's just not fun anymore."

"I felt that same way. In my entire life, I never imagined I'd retire. It had been my good fortune to work in things I really enjoyed, but the day after day started to affect me, the rules, little irritations. For example, and I know it sounds silly, but, in order to get a day off I just couldn't tell someone. There was a paper, a form, and then it wasn't even a paper, but an electronic questionnaire. Why that should have bothered me so much, I don't know."

The teacher let out a huff. "One paper? We fill out so many forms, we haven't got time for anything else."

At that point, the two of us ran out of things to say. It was if a sign went on over our heads that read, "No more chit chat. Stop talking."

The woman opened up a paperback to the midway point where she'd marked it and I looked in the other direction, out the window and, far in the distance, toward the Pacific Ocean.

Although the airplane hadn't reached my destination yet, I had. The trip was over. No more travels for me, at least for a while.

Not Long After

My Dad had a doctor's appointment, a follow-up after a fall and a cracked vertebra. Everything checked out just fine and we were driving north on Highway 41. I wasn't holding up my side of the conversation.

"What are you thinking about?" he asked.

"Flowers," I answered.

Dad gave me a look.

When my wife Anna was recuperating from her back surgery, her hospital room filled with flowers. The doctor said things went well and there was no need for her to stick around.

She went home the next day.

We took all the flowers and displayed them on the old iron stove that sits in our living room. Almost every single day, more visitors brought more flowers and pretty soon, you could barely see the stove at all.

"Friends are like flowers. When I first started to connect my thoughts on the subject, that's what popped into my head," I said.

"But nothing could be further from the truth. Flowers are beautiful, to be sure, but, in a matter of days or a week or two at the most, they wilt and begin to smell. All that is left to do is throw them away. But friends aren't like that. As time goes by, we appreciate them even more. In a way, they become prettier and smell better too."

Dad's silence made me wonder if he regretted inquiring about my thoughts.

"Maybe flowers are like moments. We collect them and, every once in a while, bring them out to smell them again, admire the colors. What do you think?"

"Sure Jim. That sounds about right."

In just the few months that had gone by since the last doctor's visit, my Dad had changed. He had an episode one weekend where he lost all contact with reality, saw water flowing out of walls and thought he was flying in an airplane when he was actually in a hospital bed.

His imagination ran wild, I guess you could say.

The most convenient explanation, reaction to medications, was ruled out and doctors checked several times just to make sure. Dementia, that's what it was. And, although Dad seemed to be better, we were all warned that it could happen again. Worse yet, this descent is irreversible.

We have grown accustomed to his begging off going certain places. "Too many memories," he will say. He insists on giving away items, ironically called memorabilia, because they evoke times he prefers not to remember.

That trip to Maine with the Moon family, for example, eludes him. When I asked about it, he shook his head. "I don't remember that."

There is no denying we are related. We have the same build, the same haircut and then there's compulsion to take center stage. But, in this one way, we are completely different. No memory could possibly be as painful for me as not being able to recall it.

"This, I will remember." That is my hope.

Made in the USA
Middletown, DE
28 September 2021